Math to Learn

A Teacher's Resource Handbook

Mary C. Cavanagh

GREAT SOURCE
EDUCATION GROUP
A Houghton Mifflin Company
New Ways to Know

M000007933

Credits:

Design and Production: Taurins Design Associates

Illustration Credits:

Creative Art: Mike Gordon
Technical Art: Taurins Design Associates

Printed in the United States of America

Great Source® and *New Ways to Know®* are registered trademarks of Houghton Mifflin Company.

International Standard Book Number -13: 978-0-669-49346-7

International Standard Book Number -10: 0-669-49346-5

5 6 7 8 9 10 MA 07

Visit our website: http://www.greatsource.com

Math to Learn is a reference handbook for students, teachers, and parents. It provides concise explanations and examples that are written on the student level. *Math to Learn*, with instructional support from teachers, is a tool that can empower students to become more responsible for their own learning, reviewing, relearning, research, and extended thinking.

TEACHER USES

Math to Learn is organized by topics, not by chapters. Some students may need only a quick review of place value concepts, but need more instruction in comparing numbers. *Math to Learn* brings all those skills together in one section.

Vocabulary is an area of mathematics that is often overlooked or not emphasized. *Math to Learn* provides an avenue for a stronger approach to terms and their applications since it contains definitions and explanations that are easy to communicate to students. The use of vocabulary in instruction also provides ways for students who have difficulty with computation to excel through their understanding of verbal relationships and meanings.

STUDENT USES

Math to Learn provides a ready reference for students when they are doing classwork or homework. There are times when textbook explanations need further clarification. *Math to Learn* gives clear explanations that allow students to understand a difficult topic more fully. The pictures, charts, and simple explanations fill gaps in learning that a student may have, but is unlikely to voice.

Student research is an important part of education. Students can easily access information in *Math to Learn* through various points of entry. They can look up a term in the glossary, found in the Yellow Pages section. The terms are cross-referenced to pages in the main section of the handbook. Each section is color coded with a key on the back cover. The use of mathematically correct vocabulary along with the examples helps students connect words with symbols. The glossary provides a comprehensive resource of math terms.

PARENT USES

Math to Learn is a concise handbook of math topics that parents can readily use. Math textbooks usually have detailed explanations of single skills. *Math to Learn* presents those single skills in a larger context and connects concepts to previous learning. Many parents may find this a useful mechanism for helping them recall mathematical steps they may have forgotten.

The wide variety of diagrams and clear explanations in *Math to Learn* gives parents a great resource to help with homework. Equipping parents to help improve their child's learning is a benefit that reaches far beyond the classroom.

The organization of this book parallels the sections of *Math to Learn*. You may first want to correlate the chapters of your textbook to the sections of *Math to Learn*. This will enable a ready reference to the practice and activities in this book. Each section may include more than one chapter of your text.

Math to Learn Teacher's Resource Book provides practice and test preparation pages for each sub-section of *Math to Learn*. These pages are followed by an answer page with answers to both the practice and test questions. Each section concludes with an application activity, designed to connect topics that relate to more than one area of mathematics.

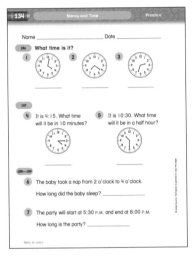

The practice pages are copymasters that follow the organization of each sub-section of *Math to Learn*. Each problem is cross-referenced to show students which page(s) in *Math to Learn* will provide help, if needed. This feature also allows you to identify specific concepts that students may need help to understand. The practice pages can be assigned by sub-section in their entirety or by question number to accompany material recently covered.

The test preparation pages are copymasters that present the concepts of each sub-section of *Math to Learn* in a variety of standardized state test formats. This enables students to become familiar with question formats they may encounter when taking standardized tests. Students who have had experience with these formats often achieve higher test scores than students who have had no prior encounters with the types of questions used in standardized tests.

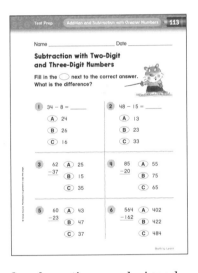

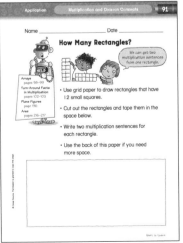

The application activities at the end of each section are designed to provide examples of mathematics as it relates to real-world situations. Some activities relate directly to daily tasks, while some involve using math manipulatives to reinforce concepts. Each application includes extension activities on the teacher page so that students may continue studies on the topic. Also included is a rubric that you may use for grading the activity.

Exploring the Handbook

OBJECTIVE
- Explore the *Math to Learn* handbook to learn the format of the book

MATERIALS
- *Math to Learn* handbook

TIME
- 20 minutes

TEACHER NOTES
- This activity helps students explore the *Math to Learn* handbook and become familiar with the organization of the handbook.

- You may wish to do this activity as a whole-class activity so that you can read the questions to the students, one question at a time.

EXTENSION
- Have students work in pairs. One student writes down an exercise which is worked out in the handbook, for example, 243 + 105 = []. The other student, using the Table of Contents and/or the Index to help, locates the page that the exercise is on. In this case, the exercise is on page 130.

ANSWERS
1. green
2. 162
3. 333
4. Addition
5. yellow
6. calculator
7. 314
8. 98

Name _____ Date _____

Exploring the Handbook

Look at the Table of Contents in the handbook. It begins on page iii.

This spot will list pages that will have information that can help you do the activity.

How to Use this Book *pages vii-ix*

1 A different color is used for each section of the book. What color is the section on Geometry? _____

2 On what page does the section on Money and Time begin? _____

Look at the Index. It is at the end of the handbook.

3 On what page does the Index begin? ____

4 What is the first word listed in the Index? _____

Look for the Glossary of Math Words. It is near the end of the book.

5 What color are the Glossary pages? _____

6 What is the first word in the Glossary that begins with the letter c? _____

7 On what page of the Glossary can you find out what the word *array* means? _____

8 If you want to know more about arrays, what page in the handbook should you go to? _____

Name _____ Date _____

Numbers to 19

2–3 Write how many.

$$0\ 1\ 2\ 3\ 4\ 5\ 6\ 7\ 8\ 9$$

1

_____

- - - - - - -

_____

2

_____

- - - - - - -

_____

3

_____

- - - - - - -

_____

4

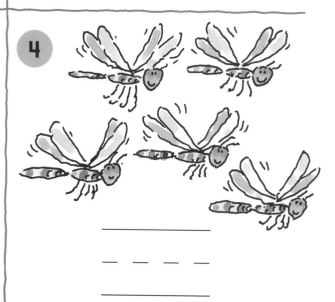

_____

- - - - - - -

_____

Name _____ Date _____

2–3 Write the number and its word name.

Word Bank
zero   one   two   three   four
five   six   seven   eight   nine

1

4   four
___ _____

2

___ _____

3

___ _____

4

___ _____

5

___ _____

6

___ _____

Name _____ Date _____

4-5 **Draw dots to match the number.**

Use the top row first.
Then use the bottom
row if you need it.

1   6

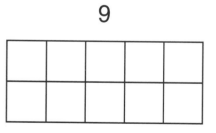

2   3

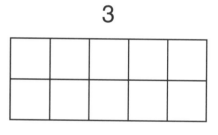

3   8

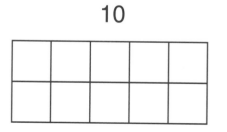

4   5

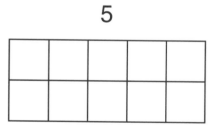

5   2

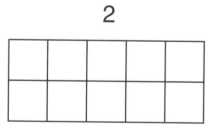

6   9

7   10

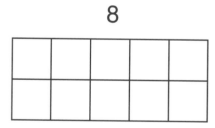

Name _____ Date _____

6–7 **Draw more dots to match the number.**

1 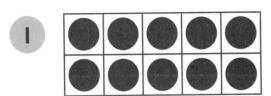 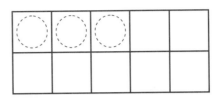 13

thirteen

2 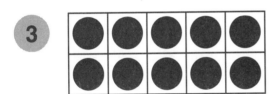 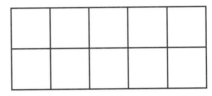 16

sixteen

3 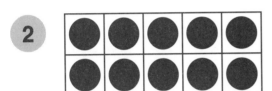 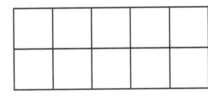 11

eleven

4 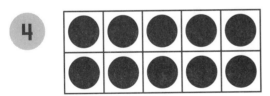 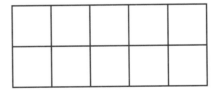 18

eighteen

5  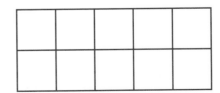 15

fifteen

Name _____ Date _____

6–7 **Write the number and its word name.**

Word Bank

seventeen	thirteen	twelve
nineteen	fifteen	fourteen

1

15
fifteen

2 _____

_____

3 _____

_____

4 _____

_____

5 _____

_____

Name _____ Date _____

2–7 **Fill in the missing numbers.**

1

0	1	2	3		5	6		8	9
10	11		13	14			17		19

2 7 8 9 _____ 11 12 13 _____ 15 _____

Write the numeral.

3 two ___2___

4 zero _____

5 seventeen _____

6 three _____

Write the missing letter.

7 8 eigh_t_

8 5 ___ive

9 10 t___n

10 11 ele___en

Name _____ Date _____

Numbers to 19

Write how many.

 1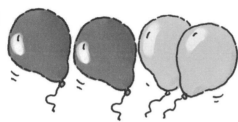

_____

– – – – – – –

_____

2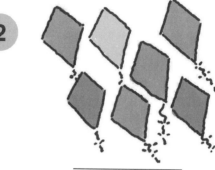

_____

– – – – – – –

_____

3

_____

– – – – – – –

_____

4

_____

– – – – – – –

_____

5

_____

– – – – – – –

_____

6

_____

– – – – – – –

_____

Name _____ Date _____

Numbers to 19

Fill in the ⬭ next to the correct answer.

1 How many dots?

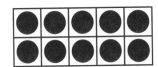

  A 17   **B** 12   **C** 14   **D** 16

---

2 How many dots?

  A fourteen   **B** seventeen

  C fifteen   **D** twelve

---

3 What number is missing?

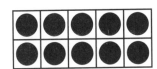

9	10	11		13

  A 17   **B** 12

  C 15   **D** 14

4 What number is missing?

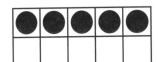

16	17		19

  A 14   **B** 16

  C 15   **D** 18

PRACTICE ANSWERS

Page 8

1. 6   2. 3
3. 7   4. 5

Page 9

1. 4 four   2. 7 seven
3. 2 two   4. 1 one
5. 9 nine   6. 5 five

Page 10

1.
2.
3.
4.
5.
6.
7.

Page 11

1.
2.
3.
4.
5.

Page 12

1. 15 fifteen
2. 12 twelve
3. 17 seventeen
4. 19 nineteen
5. 14 fourteen

Page 13

1. 1st row: 4, 7
   2nd row: 12, 15, 16, 18
2. 10, 14, 16
3. 2   4. 0
5. 17   6. 3
7. t   8. f
9. e   10. v

TEST PREP ANSWERS

Page 14

1. 4
2. 7
3. 9
4. 8
5. 10
6. 6

Page 15

1. B
2. C
3. B
4. D

Name _____ Date _____

8　Place Value to 1000

0	1	2	3	4	5	6	7	8	9
10	11	12	13	14	15	16	17	18	19
20	21	22	23	24	25	26	27	28	29
30	31	32	33	34	35	36	37	38	39
40	41	42	43	44	45	46	47	48	49
50	51	52	53	54	55	56	57	58	59
60	61	62	63	64	65	66	67	68	69
70	71	72	73	74	75	76	77	78	79
80	81	82	83	84	85	86	87	88	89
90	91	92	93	94	95	96	97	98	99

1　Circle the numbers that have 4 tens.

2　Color the squares that have a number with 4 ones.

3　Which number has 4 tens and 4 ones? _____

Name _____ Date _____

8   **Fill in the missing numbers. Look for patterns.**

0	1	2	3	4	5			8	9
10	11	12	13				17		
20	21		23					28	29
		33				36			
	41			45	46			48	
50		52		55					59
		63				67			
70		73			76				79
	81		84						
		92				96			99

Name _____ Date _____

 9–13 **Write how many.**

1

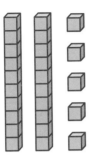

Tens	Ones
2	5

25

2

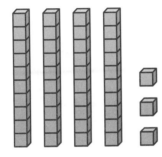

Tens	Ones

_____

3

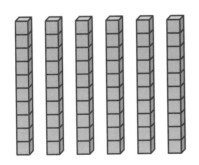

Tens	Ones

_____

4

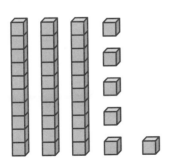

Tens	Ones

_____

Name _____ Date _____

14 **Write the numeral for the word name.**

1 fifty-two ___52___

2 twenty-four _____

3 fifty _____

4 sixty-one _____

5 seventy-six _____

6 eighty-five _____

15 *Write About Math*

7 How are 36 and 63 alike?

_____

_____

_____

8 How are 36 and 63 different?

_____

_____

_____

Name _____ Date _____

16–17 **Here are 100 ladybugs.**

1 Circle groups of 10.

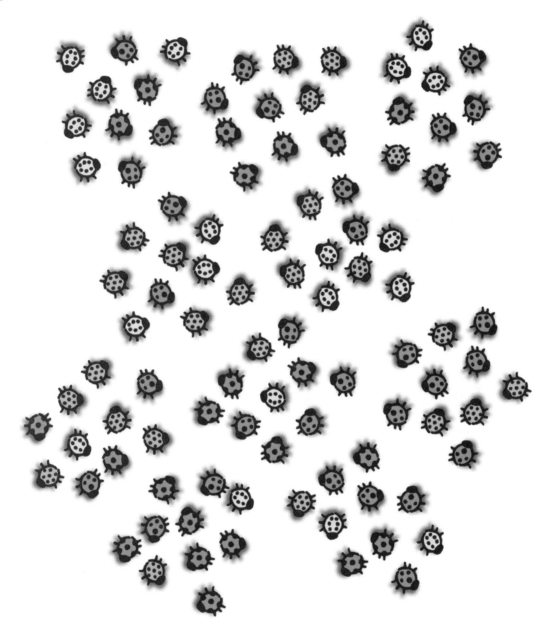

2 How many groups of 10 are there? _____

Name _____ Date _____

18–21   **Write how many.**

1 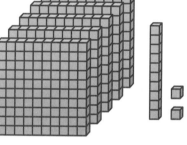

Hundreds	Tens	Ones
2	3	5

_____

2 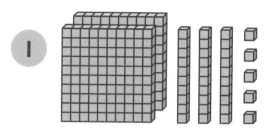

Hundreds	Tens	Ones

_____

3 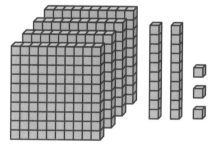

Hundreds	Tens	Ones

_____

4 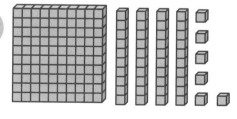

Hundreds	Tens	Ones

_____

Name _____ Date _____

22-23 **Write how many.**

1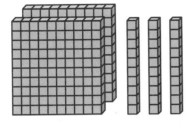

Hundreds	Tens	Ones
2	3	0

_____

2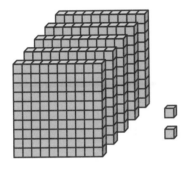

Hundreds	Tens	Ones

_____

3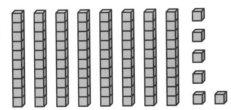

Hundreds	Tens	Ones

_____

24 **Write the number.**

4 When you count to 9, the next number is _____.

5 When you count to 99, the next number is _____.

6 When you count to 999, the next number is _____.

Name _____ Date _____

Place Value to 1000

1 Fill in the missing numbers on the number chart.

0	1	2		4	5		7		9
10	11		13	14	15		17		
20		22	23			26			29
	31		33			36			

2 Look at the bottom row on the number chart.
What number is in the tens place? _____

Write how many.

3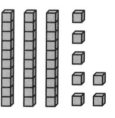

Tens	Ones

_____

4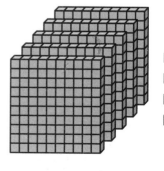

Hundreds	Tens	Ones

_____

Name _____ Date _____

Place Value to 1000

Fill in the ⬭ next to the correct answer.

How many?

1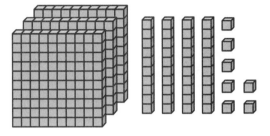

    Ⓐ 47   Ⓑ 743

    Ⓒ 347   Ⓓ 37

2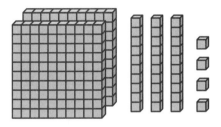

    Ⓐ 204   Ⓑ 234

    Ⓒ 203   Ⓓ 230

3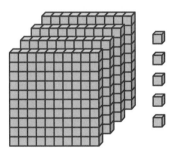

    Ⓐ 45   Ⓑ 450

    Ⓒ 504   Ⓓ 405

4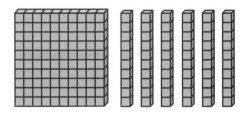

    Ⓐ 160   Ⓑ 16

    Ⓒ 61   Ⓓ 106

PRACTICE ANSWERS
Page 17

1. and 2.

0	1	2	3	4	5	6	7	8	9
10	11	12	13	14	15	16	17	18	19
20	21	22	23	24	25	26	27	28	29
30	31	32	33	34	35	36	37	38	39
40	41	42	43	44	45	46	47	48	49
50	51	52	53	54	55	56	57	58	59
60	61	62	63	64	65	66	67	68	69
70	71	72	73	74	75	76	77	78	79
80	81	82	83	84	85	86	87	88	89
90	91	92	93	94	95	96	97	98	99

3. 44

Page 18

1st row: 6, 7

2nd row: 14, 15, 16, 18, 19

3rd row: 22, 24, 25, 26, 27

4th row: 30, 31, 32, 34, 35, 37, 38, 39

5th row: 40, 42, 43, 44, 47, 49

6th row: 51, 53, 54, 56, 57, 58

7th row: 60, 61, 62, 64, 65, 66, 68, 69

8th row: 71, 72, 74, 74, 77, 78

9th row: 80, 82, 83, 85, 86, 87, 88, 89

10th row: 90, 91, 93, 94, 95, 97, 98

Page 19

1.

Tens	Ones
2	5

25

2.

Tens	Ones
4	3

43

3.

Tens	Ones
6	0

60

4.

Tens	Ones
3	6

36

Page 20

1. 52   **2.** 24

3. 50   **4.** 61

5. 76   **6.** 85

7. Answers will vary. Possible answer: 36 and 63 both have the same digits, 3 and 6.

8. Answers will vary. Possible answer: 36 and 63 have different values. 36 has 3 tens and 6 ones. 63 has 6 tens and 3 ones.

Page 21

1. Check students' work. They should have drawn 10 circles with 10 ladybugs in each circle.

2. 10

Page 22

1.

Hundreds	Tens	Ones
2	3	5

235

2.

Hundreds	Tens	Ones
5	1	2

512

3.

Hundreds	Tens	Ones
4	2	3

423

4.

Hundreds	Tens	Ones
1	4	6

146

Page 23

1.

Hundreds	Tens	Ones
2	3	0

230

2.

Hundreds	Tens	Ones
5	0	2

502

3.

Hundreds	Tens	Ones
0	8	6

86

4. 10

5. 100

6. 1000

TEST PREP ANSWERS
Page 24

1. 1st row: 3, 6, 8

2nd row: 12, 16, 18, 19

3rd row: 21, 24, 25, 27, 28

4th row: 30, 32, 34, 35, 37, 38, 39

2. 3

3.

Tens	Ones
3	7

37

4.

Hundreds	Tens	Ones
5	0	4

504

Page 25

1. C

2. B

3. D

4. A

Name _____ **Date** _____

Compare and Order Numbers

26–27 **Write how many. Circle the greater number.**

1

_____   _____

2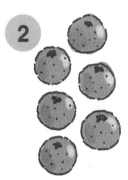

_____   _____

3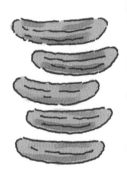

_____   _____

4

_____   _____

5

_____   _____

6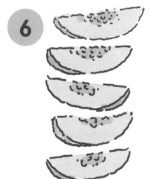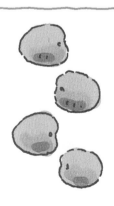

_____   _____

Name _____ Date _____

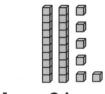

26 **is greater than** 14.
26 > 14

14 **is less than** 26.
14 < 26

26–31 Write < or > in the ◯ .

1 5 ◯ 2

2 7 ◯ 10

3 8 ◯ 3

4 27 ◯ 40

5 64 ◯ 33

6 90 ◯ 89

7 61 ◯ 9

8 18 ◯ 45

9 71 ◯ 56

10 34 ◯ 73

11 163 ◯ 200

12 308 ◯ 855

13 726 ◯ 591

14 275 ◯ 99

15 462 ◯ 426

16 571 ◯ 581

Name _____ Date _____

32–33 **Write the counting number that goes between.**

1 6 _____ 8

2 3 _____ 5

3 9 _____ 11

4 13 _____ 15

5 64 _____ 66

6 79 _____ 81

Write the counting number that comes just after.

7 5 _____

8 9 _____

9 7 _____

10 1 _____

11 14 _____

12 28 _____

13 53 _____

14 19 _____

Write the counting number that comes just before.

15 _____ 8

16 _____ 5

17 _____ 2

18 _____ 7

19 _____ 17

20 _____ 26

21 _____ 30

22 _____ 53

Name _____ Date _____

34 **Write the numbers in order from least to greatest.**

1 | 4 | 8 | 1 |

_____ _____ _____

2 | 9 | 3 | 6 |

_____ _____ _____

3 | 7 | 15 | 12 |

_____ _____ _____

4 | 23 | 18 | 31 |

_____ _____ _____

35

Tom Sally Kirk Sean Allie Lisa Jan

5 Who is first in line? _____

6 Who is 3rd in line? _____

7 Who is fifth in line? _____

36–37 **Tell whether the number is odd or even.**

8 5 _____

9 4 _____

10 32 _____

11 47 _____

Name _____ Date _____

Compare and Order Numbers

Write < or > in the ◯.

1 4 ◯ 7   **2** 6 ◯ 2

3 24 ◯ 22   **4** 32 ◯ 21

5 70 ◯ 68   **6** 441 ◯ 490

Write the counting number that goes between.

7 3 _____ 5   **8** 14 _____ 16

Write the counting number that comes just after.

9 6 _____   **10** 18 _____

Write the counting number that comes just before.

11 _____ 5   **12** _____ 10

Write the numbers in order from least to greatest.

13 | 6 | 9 | 4 | **14** | 17 | 12 | 23 |

_____ _____ _____   _____ _____ _____

PRACTICE ANSWERS

Page 27

1. 2 ③
2. ⑥ 4
3. ⑨ 5
4. ⑧ 3
5. 4 ⑦
6. ⑤ 4

Page 28

1. >	2. <
3. >	4. <
5. >	6. >
7. >	8. <
9. >	10. <
11. <	12. <
13. >	14. >
15. >	16. <

Page 29

1. 7	2. 4
3. 10	4. 14
5. 65	6. 80
7. 6	8. 10
9. 8	10. 2
11. 15	12. 29
13. 54	14. 20
15. 7	16. 4
17. 1	18. 6
19. 16	20. 25
21. 29	22. 52

Page 30

1. 1, 4, 8 2. 3, 6, 9
3. 7, 12, 15 4. 18, 23, 31
5. Tom
6. Kirk
7. Allie
8. odd
9. even
10. even
11. odd

TEST PREP ANSWERS

Page 31

1. <	2. >
3. >	4. >
5. >	6. <
7. 4	8. 15
9. 7	10. 19
11. 4	12. 9
13. 4, 6, 9	14. 12, 17, 23

Name _____ Date _____

Estimation

40–41 **Round each number to the nearest ten.**

1 12 rounds to _____.   **2** 15 rounds to _____.

3 19 rounds to _____.   **4** 14 rounds to _____.

5 31 rounds to _____.   **6** 34 rounds to _____.

7 35 rounds to _____.   **8** 38 rounds to _____.

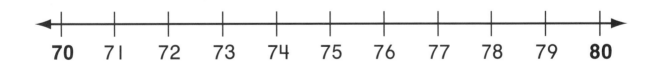

9 77 rounds to _____.   **10** 73 rounds to _____.

11 71 rounds to _____.   **12** 75 rounds to _____.

Name _____ Date _____

41 **Round each number to the nearest hundred.**

1 130 rounds to _____.   **2** 172 rounds to _____.

3 151 rounds to _____.   **4** 148 rounds to _____.

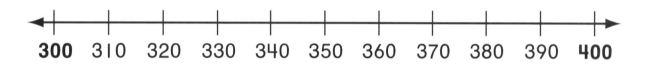

5 309 rounds to _____.   **6** 346 rounds to _____.

7 350 rounds to _____.   **8** 382 rounds to _____.

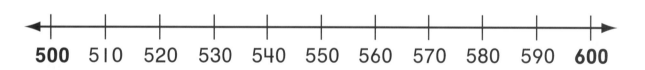

9 586 rounds to _____.   **10** 555 rounds to _____.

11 537 rounds to _____.   **12** 528 rounds to _____.

Math to Learn

Name _____ Date _____

Estimation

Fill in the ⬭ next to the correct answer.

Round to the nearest ten.

10   11   12   13   14   15   16   17   18   19   **20**

1   17 rounds to _____.

(A) 10   (B) 20

2   12 rounds to _____.

(A) 10   (B) 20

3   13 rounds to _____.

(A) 10   (B) 20

4   15 rounds to _____.

(A) 10   (B) 20

Round to the nearest hundred.

100   110   120   130   140   150   160   170   180   190   **200**

5   158 rounds to _____.

(A) 100   (B) 200

6   143 rounds to _____.

(A) 100   (B) 200

PRACTICE ANSWERS
Page 33

1. 10
2. 20
3. 20
4. 10
5. 30
6. 30
7. 40
8. 40
9. 80
10. 70
11. 70
12. 80

Page 34

1. 100
2. 200
3. 200
4. 100
5. 300
6. 300
7. 400
8. 400
9. 600
10. 600
11. 500
12. 500

TEST PREP ANSWERS
Page 35

1. B
2. A
3. A
4. B
5. B
6. A

Name _____ Date _____

Fractions

42–43 Circle the figures that show halves.
Color $\frac{1}{2}$ of each of those figures red.

1 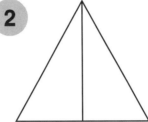 **2** 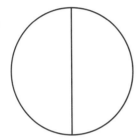 **3**

4  **5** 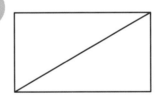 **6**

7 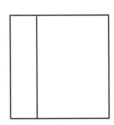 **8** 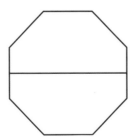 **9**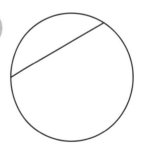

Name _____ Date _____

44–45 Color $\frac{1}{3}$ of each shape orange.

1    **2** 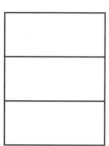   **3**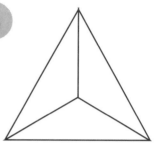

46–47 Color $\frac{1}{4}$ of each shape green.

4 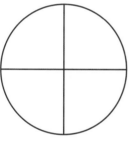   **5**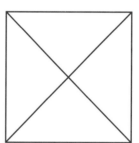

6

Name _____ Date _____

44–49 **Use the pictures.**

1 Circle pictures that show $\frac{2}{3}$ shaded.

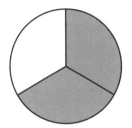 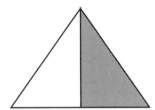 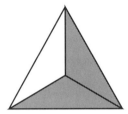

2 Color 2 bugs.

What fraction of the bugs did you color? _____

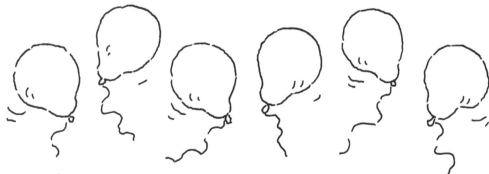

3 Color $\frac{1}{6}$ of the balloons red.

4 Color $\frac{2}{6}$ of the balloons yellow.

5 Color three sixths of the balloons blue.

Math to Learn

Name _____ Date _____

50–51 **Write a fraction for each shaded amount.**

Write <, >, or = in each **.**

1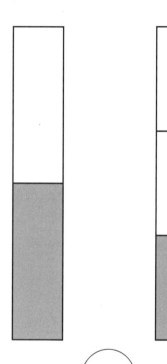

_____ ◯ _____

2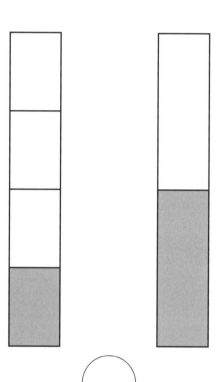

_____ ◯ _____

3

_____ ◯ _____

Name _____ Date _____

Fractions

Fill in the ⬭ next to the correct answer.

Name the fraction that is shaded.

1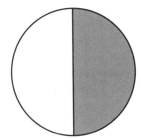

 A $\frac{1}{3}$ **B** $\frac{1}{4}$

C $\frac{1}{2}$ **D** $\frac{2}{3}$

2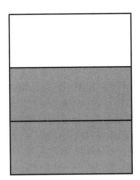

 A $\frac{2}{3}$ **B** $\frac{1}{4}$

C $\frac{3}{2}$ **D** $\frac{3}{4}$

3

 A $\frac{3}{4}$ **B** $\frac{2}{4}$

C $\frac{1}{2}$ **D** $\frac{2}{3}$

Math to Learn

Name _____ Date _____

Fractions

1 Color $\frac{1}{2}$ of the circle.

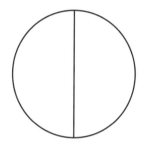

2 Color $\frac{2}{3}$ of the circle.

3 Color $\frac{2}{3}$ of the balloons.

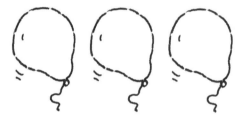

4 Write a fraction for each shaded amount.

Write >, <, or = in the ◯.

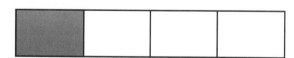

PRACTICE ANSWERS
Page 37
1.–9. 1, 2, 4, 5, and 8 should be circled. Half of each of the circled figures should be colored red.

Page 38
1.–3. For each shape, one third of the shape should be colored orange.

4.–6. For each shape, one fourth of the shape should be colored green.

Page 39
1. The first and third pictures should be circled.

2. Two of the bugs should be colored. $\frac{2}{3}$

3.–5. 1 balloon should be colored red. 2 balloons should be colored yellow. 3 balloons should be colored blue.

Page 40
1. $\frac{1}{2} > \frac{1}{3}$

2. $\frac{1}{4} < \frac{1}{2}$

3. $\frac{1}{4} < \frac{1}{3}$ or $\frac{1}{3} > \frac{1}{4}$

TEST PREP ANSWERS
Page 41
1. C

2. A

3. A

Page 42
1. One of the two equal parts should be shaded.

2. Two of the three equal parts should be shaded.

3. Two of the balloons should be shaded.

4. $\frac{1}{2} > \frac{1}{4}$ or $\frac{1}{4} < \frac{1}{2}$

Dog Show

OBJECTIVES
- Write whole numbers through 99
- Compare and order whole numbers through 99
- Make an organized list of numbers

MATERIALS
- pencil and paper

TIME
- 30–40 minutes

TEACHER NOTES
- Read the task to the students.

- Be sure students understand the terms *digit* and *two-digit numbers*.

- Show students how to use the digits, 2, 3, 5, and 8 to make the dogs' numbers.

- Point out to students that they may use the same digit twice to make a two-digit number (for example, 22 or 33).

- Ask questions such as:

  What are some possible numbers for the dogs?

  How can you put the numbers in order from least to greatest?

  How can you find all the possible numbers?

EXTENSIONS
- Have students make up their own word problems using the same or different digits.

- Have students write about how they organized the numbers.

ANSWERS
There are 16 possible two-digit numbers.

Listed from least to greatest, the numbers are: 22, 23, 25, 28, 32, 33, 35, 38, 52, 53, 55, 58, 82, 83, 85, and 88.

You may wish to use this **scoring rubric** to assess students' work.

3 points	• Student develops and executes a plan to make a list of all the possible two-digit numbers. • Student writes at least 14 of the possible 16 two-digit numbers. • Student correctly writes the numbers in order from least to greatest.
2 points	• Student writes between 5 and 13 of the possible two-digit numbers and writes the numbers in order from least to greatest with few or no errors. • Student writes 14 or more of the numbers but is unable to correctly order them from least to greatest.
1 point	• Student writes fewer than 5 of the possible two-digit numbers. • Student writes 5 to 13 of the numbers but makes many errors in ordering the numbers.

Name _____ Date _____

Numbers to 99
pages 8–15

Comparing and
Ordering Numbers
pages 26–34

Dog Show

You and your friends are having a dog show. You have to make a number for each dog.

• Each dog will need a two-digit number.

• You may only use the digits **2**, **3**, **5**, and **8** to make the dogs' numbers.

• Write all the possible numbers the dogs can get.

• Write the numbers in order from least to greatest.

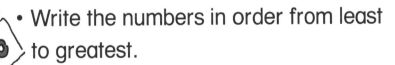

Name _____ Date _____

Addition

54–56 **Write how many in each group.**
Write how many in all.

1

$$\underline{3} + \underline{2} = \underline{5}$$
in all

2

$$\underline{} + \underline{} = \underline{}$$
in all

3

$$\underline{} + \underline{} = \underline{}$$
in all

4

$$\underline{} + \underline{} = \underline{}$$
in all

5

$$\underline{} + \underline{} = \underline{}$$
in all

6

$$\underline{} + \underline{} = \underline{}$$
in all

Name _____ Date _____

$$3 + 2 = 5$$

$$3 + 2 = 5$$

57   **Draw to show each addend. Write the sum.**

1

$$4 + 1 = \underline{\hspace{1cm}}$$

2

$$2 + 2 = \underline{\hspace{1cm}}$$

3

$$1 + 5 = \underline{\hspace{1cm}}$$

4

$$4 + 3 = \underline{\hspace{1cm}}$$

5

$$5 + 2 = \underline{\hspace{1cm}}$$

6

$$2 + 1 = \underline{\hspace{1cm}}$$

Name _____ Date _____

$$7 + 2 = 9$$
$$\text{or}$$
$$2 + 7 = 9$$

58–61 **Count on to find the first sum.**
Use the first sum to find the next sum.

1 $4 + 2 = $ ____

$2 + 4 = $ ____

2 $8 + 1 = $ ____

$1 + 8 = $ ____

3 $5 + 3 = $ ____

$3 + 5 = $ ____

4 $7 + 1 = $ ____

$1 + 7 = $ ____

5 $6 + 2 = $ ____

$2 + 6 = $ ____

6 $8 + 3 = $ ____

$3 + 8 = $ ____

7 $9 + 3 = $ ____

$3 + 9 = $ ____

8 $5 + 2 = $ ____

$2 + 5 = $ ____

9 $6 + 1 = $ ____

$1 + 6 = $ ____

10 $4 + 3 = $ ____

$3 + 4 = $ ____

11 $7 + 3 = $ ____

$3 + 7 = $ ____

12 $5 + 0 = $ ____

$0 + 5 = $ ____

Name _____   Date _____

Write each sum.

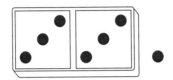

1 3 + 3 = ____

3 + 4 = ____

4 + 3 = ____

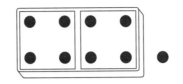

2 4 + 4 = ____

4 + 5 = ____

5 + 4 = ____

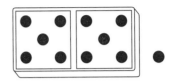

3 5 + 5 = ____

5 + 6 = ____

6 + 5 = ____

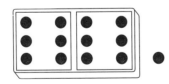

4 6 + 6 = ____

6 + 7 = ____

7 + 6 = ____

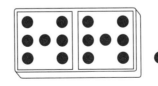

5 7 + 7 = ____

7 + 8 = ____

8 + 7 = ____

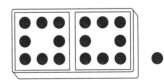

6 8 + 8 = ____

8 + 9 = ____

9 + 8 = ____

Name _____ Date _____

64, 67 **Fill the ten frame. Write the addends.**

1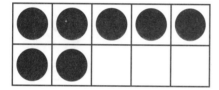

___9___ + ___1___ = 10

2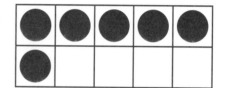

_____ + _____ = 10

3

_____ + _____ = 10

4

_____ + _____ = 10

Write four different ways to make 10.

5 _____ + _____ = 10   _____ + _____ = 10

_____ + _____ = 10   _____ + _____ = 10

Write About Math

6 Tell a math story about 3 + 7 = 10.

_____

_____

Name _____ Date _____

64 Fill the ten frame. Put the extras outside.
Write the sum.

1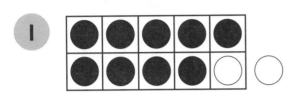

$9 + 2 = $ ___

2

$8 + 4 = $ ___

3

$5 + 6 = $ ___

4

$7 + 5 = $ ___

5

$9 + 3 = $ ___

6

$9 + 4 = $ ___

65 Write each sum.

7 $9 + 2 = $ ___ **8** $5 + 9 = $ ___ **9** $9 + 6 = $ ___

10 $7 + 9 = $ ___ **11** $9 + 8 = $ ___ **12** $9 + 9 = $ ___

13 $4 + 9 = $ ___ **14** $6 + 9 = $ ___ **15** $3 + 9 = $ ___

Math to Learn

Name _____ Date _____

66 **Fill the five frame. Write the addends.**

1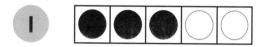

$\underline{3} + \underline{2} = 5$

2

$\underline{} + \underline{} = 5$

3

$\underline{} + \underline{} = 5$

4

$\underline{} + \underline{} = 5$

Fill the five frame.
Put the extras outside.
Write the sum.

5

$4 + 2 = \underline{6}$

6

$3 + 4 = \underline{}$

7

$2 + 5 = \underline{}$

8

$2 + 4 = \underline{}$

Math to Learn

Name _____ Date _____

68–69   **Write the sums in the addition table.**

+	0	1	2	3	4	5
0	0 + 0	0 + 1	0 + 2	0 + 3	0 + 4	0 + 5
	___	___	___	___	___	___
1	1 + 0	1 + 1	1 + 2	1 + 3	1 + 4	1 + 5
	___	___	___	___	___	___
2	2 + 0	2 + 1	2 + 2	2 + 3	2 + 4	2 + 5
	___	___	___	___	___	___
3	3 + 0	3 + 1	3 + 2	3 + 3	3 + 4	3 + 5
	___	___	___	7	___	___
4	4 + 0	4 + 1	4 + 2	4 + 3	4 + 4	4 + 5
	___	___	___	___	___	___
5	5 + 0	5 + 1	5 + 2	5 + 3	5 + 4	5 + 5
	___	___	___	___	___	___

Name _____ Date _____

70–71 **Add. Look for easy facts.**
Draw a line under the first two numbers you add.

1 $3 + 5 + 1 =$ _____

2 $6 + 1 + 2 =$ _____

3 $4 + 2 + 2 =$ _____

4 $3 + 4 + 3 =$ _____

5 $2 + 3 + 1 + 3 =$ _____

6 $4 + 2 + 1 + 3 =$ _____

7
2
3
+ 2

8
1
6
+ 3

9
2
3
+ 4

10
1
1
+ 7

11
3
1
+ 5

Look for numbers
that make 10.

12
8
3
+ 2

13
3
5
+ 5

14
6
5
+ 4

15
3
7
+ 8

16
9
1
+ 4

Name _____ Date _____

54–69 Write the sums.
Cross out the facts you know.
Keep track of facts you need to study.

Add 1	Add 2	Add 3	Add 4
0 + 1 = ___	0 + 2 = ___	0 + 3 = ___	0 + 4 = ___
1 + 1 = ___	1 + 2 = ___	1 + 3 = ___	1 + 4 = ___
2 + 1 = ___	2 + 2 = ___	2 + 3 = ___	2 + 4 = ___
3 + 1 = ___	3 + 2 = ___	3 + 3 = ___	3 + 4 = ___
4 + 1 = ___	4 + 2 = ___	4 + 3 = ___	4 + 4 = ___
5 + 1 = ___	5 + 2 = ___	5 + 3 = ___	5 + 4 = ___
6 + 1 = ___	6 + 2 = ___	6 + 3 = ___	6 + 4 = ___
7 + 1 = ___	7 + 2 = ___	7 + 3 = ___	7 + 4 = ___
8 + 1 = ___	8 + 2 = ___	8 + 3 = ___	8 + 4 = ___
9 + 1 = ___	9 + 2 = ___	9 + 3 = ___	9 + 4 = ___

Name _____ Date _____

Write the sums.
Cross out the facts you know.
Keep track of facts you need to study.

Add 5	Add 6	Add 7	Add 8
0 + 5 = ____	0 + 6 = ____	0 + 7 = ____	0 + 8 = ____
1 + 5 = ____	1 + 6 = ____	1 + 7 = ____	1 + 8 = ____
2 + 5 = ____	2 + 6 = ____	2 + 7 = ____	2 + 8 = ____
3 + 5 = ____	3 + 6 = ____	3 + 7 = ____	3 + 8 = ____
4 + 5 = ____	4 + 6 = ____	4 + 7 = ____	4 + 8 = ____
5 + 5 = ____	5 + 6 = ____	5 + 7 = ____	5 + 8 = ____
6 + 5 = ____	6 + 6 = ____	6 + 7 = ____	6 + 8 = ____
7 + 5 = ____	7 + 6 = ____	7 + 7 = ____	7 + 8 = ____
8 + 5 = ____	8 + 6 = ____	8 + 7 = ____	8 + 8 = ____
9 + 5 = ____	9 + 6 = ____	9 + 7 = ____	9 + 8 = ____

Name _____ Date _____

Addition

Write how many in each group.
Write how many in all.

1

____ + ____ = ____

in all

2

____ + ____ = ____

in all

Fill the five frame. Write the addends.

3

____ + ____ = 5

4

____ + ____ = 5

5 8 + 1 = ___

1 + 8 = ___

6 5 + 2 = ___

2 + 5 = ___

7 7 + 3 = ___

3 + 7 = ___

8 Draw to show each addend.
Write the sum.

4 + 3 = ____

Name _____ Date _____

Addition

Fill in the ⬭ next to the correct answer.

What is the sum?

1 8 + 3 = _____

  (A) 9   (B) 10

  (C) 11   (D) 12

2 6 + 4 = _____

  (A) 9   (B) 10

  (C) 11   (D) 12

3 7 + 7 = _____

  (A) 14   (B) 12

  (C) 15   (D) 13

4 7 + 8 = _____

  (A) 13   (B) 11

  (C) 14   (D) 15

5 4 + 7 + 6 = _____

  (A) 14   (B) 15

  (C) 17   (D) 16

6
  3
  4
  2
  + 7
  ___

  (A) 14

  (B) 16

  (C) 15

  (D) 18

PRACTICE ANSWERS
Page 46

1. $3 + 2 = 5$ **2.** $1 + 3 = 4$
3. $4 + 1 = 5$ **4.** $2 + 2 = 4$
5. $4 + 4 = 8$ **6.** $2 + 3 = 5$

Page 47

Possible student drawings are shown.

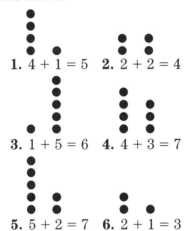

1. $4 + 1 = 5$ **2.** $2 + 2 = 4$

3. $1 + 5 = 6$ **4.** $4 + 3 = 7$

5. $5 + 2 = 7$ **6.** $2 + 1 = 3$

Page 48

1. 6, 6 **2.** 9, 9 **3.** 8, 8
4. 8, 8 **5.** 8, 8 **6.** 11, 11
7. 12, 12 **8.** 7, 7 **9.** 7, 7
10. 7, 7 **11.** 10, 10 **12.** 5, 5

Page 49

1. 6	**2.** 8	**3.** 10
7	9	11
7	9	11
4. 12	**5.** 14	**6.** 16
13	15	17
13	15	17

Page 50

1. $9 + 1 = 10$
2. $8 + 2 = 10$
3. $7 + 3 = 10$
4. $6 + 4 = 10$

5. Answers will vary. The list of possible answers are:
$0 + 10 = 10$
$1 + 9 = 10$
$2 + 8 = 10$
$3 + 7 = 10$
$4 + 6 = 10$
$5 + 5 = 10$
$6 + 4 = 10$
$7 + 3 = 10$
$8 + 2 = 10$
$9 + 1 = 10$
$10 + 0 = 10$

6. Answers will vary. Sample answer: Troy has 3 fish. He bought 7 more fish. Now he has 10 fish.

Page 51

1. 11 **2.** 12
3. 11 **4.** 12
5. 12 **6.** 13
7. 11 **8.** 14 **9.** 15
10. 16 **11.** 17 **12.** 18
13. 13 **14.** 15 **15.** 12

Page 52

1. $3 + 2 = 5$ **2.** $4 + 1 = 5$
3. $1 + 4 = 5$ **4.** $2 + 3 = 5$
5. 6 **6.** 7
7. 7 **8.** 6

Page 53

+	0	1	2	3	4	5
0	$0+0$ $\underline{0}$	$0+1$ $\underline{1}$	$0+2$ $\underline{2}$	$0+3$ $\underline{3}$	$0+4$ $\underline{4}$	$0+5$ $\underline{5}$
1	$1+0$ $\underline{1}$	$1+1$ 2	$1+2$ 3	$1+3$ 4	$1+4$ 5	$1+5$ 6
2	$2+0$ 2	$2+1$ 3	$2+2$ 4	$2+3$ 5	$2+4$ 6	$2+5$ 7
3	$3+0$ 3	$3+1$ 4	$3+2$ 5	$3+3$ 6	$3+4$ 7	$3+5$ 8
4	$4+0$ 4	$4+1$ 5	$4+2$ 6	$4+3$ 7	$4+4$ 8	$4+5$ 9
5	$5+0$ 5	$5+1$ 6	$5+2$ 7	$5+3$ 8	$5+4$ 9	$5+5$ $\underline{10}$

Page 54

1. 9 **2.** 9
3. 8 **4.** 10
5. 9 **6.** 10
7. 7 **8.** 10
9. 9 **10.** 9
11. 9 **12.** 13
13. 13 **14.** 15
15. 18 **16.** 14

Page 55

Add 1	Add 2	Add 3	Add 4
$0 + 1 = \underline{1}$	$0 + 2 = 2$	$0 + 3 = 3$	$0 + 4 = \underline{4}$
$1 + 1 = \underline{2}$	$1 + 2 = 3$	$1 + 3 = \underline{4}$	$1 + 4 = \underline{5}$
$2 + 1 = \underline{3}$	$2 + 2 = \underline{4}$	$2 + 3 = \underline{5}$	$2 + 4 = \underline{6}$
$3 + 1 = \underline{4}$	$3 + 2 = 5$	$3 + 3 = \underline{6}$	$3 + 4 = \underline{7}$
$4 + 1 = \underline{5}$	$4 + 2 = \underline{6}$	$4 + 3 = \underline{7}$	$4 + 4 = 8$
$5 + 1 = \underline{6}$	$5 + 2 = \underline{7}$	$5 + 3 = 8$	$5 + 4 = 9$
$6 + 1 = \underline{7}$	$6 + 2 = 8$	$6 + 3 = 9$	$6 + 4 = \underline{10}$
$7 + 1 = \underline{8}$	$7 + 2 = 9$	$7 + 3 = \underline{10}$	$7 + 4 = \underline{11}$
$8 + 1 = \underline{9}$	$8 + 2 = \underline{10}$	$8 + 3 = \underline{11}$	$8 + 4 = \underline{12}$
$9 + 1 = \underline{10}$	$9 + 2 = \underline{11}$	$9 + 3 = \underline{12}$	$9 + 4 = \underline{13}$

Page 56

Add 5	Add 6	Add 7	Add 8
$0 + 5 = \underline{5}$	$0 + 6 = \underline{6}$	$0 + 7 = \underline{7}$	$0 + 8 = \underline{8}$
$1 + 5 = \underline{6}$	$1 + 6 = \underline{7}$	$1 + 7 = \underline{8}$	$1 + 8 = \underline{9}$
$2 + 5 = \underline{7}$	$2 + 6 = \underline{8}$	$2 + 7 = \underline{9}$	$2 + 8 = \underline{10}$
$3 + 5 = \underline{8}$	$3 + 6 = \underline{9}$	$3 + 7 = \underline{10}$	$3 + 8 = \underline{11}$
$4 + 5 = \underline{9}$	$4 + 6 = \underline{10}$	$4 + 7 = \underline{11}$	$4 + 8 = \underline{12}$
$5 + 5 = \underline{10}$	$5 + 6 = \underline{11}$	$5 + 7 = \underline{12}$	$5 + 8 = \underline{13}$
$6 + 5 = \underline{11}$	$6 + 6 = \underline{12}$	$6 + 7 = \underline{13}$	$6 + 8 = \underline{14}$
$7 + 5 = \underline{12}$	$7 + 6 = \underline{13}$	$7 + 7 = \underline{14}$	$7 + 8 = \underline{15}$
$8 + 5 = \underline{13}$	$8 + 6 = \underline{14}$	$8 + 7 = \underline{15}$	$8 + 8 = \underline{16}$
$9 + 5 = \underline{14}$	$9 + 6 = \underline{15}$	$9 + 7 = \underline{16}$	$9 + 8 = \underline{17}$

TEST PREP ANSWERS
Page 57

1. $3 + 2 = 5$ **2.** $4 + 3 = 7$
3. $3 + 2 = 5$ **4.** $4 + 1 = 5$
5. 9, 9 **6.** 7, 7 **7.** 10, 10
8. ● ● ● ●   ● ● ● 7

Page 58

1. C **2.** B
3. A **4.** D
5. C **6.** B

Name _____ Date _____

Subtraction

72–73 Write how many in all. Write how many go away. Write how many are left.

1

_5_ – _3_ = _2_

are left

2

_____ – _____ = _____

are left

3

_____ – _____ = _____

are left

4

_____ – _____ = _____

are left

5

_____ – _____ = _____

are left

6

_____ – _____ = _____

are left

Name _____ Date _____

Whole
○ ○ ○ ○ ○

Part	Part
● ●	● ● ●

$$5 - 2 = 3$$

---

74 **Find the missing part.**

1
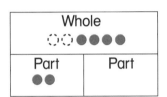

Whole
○ ○ ● ● ● ●
Part	Part
● ●	

$$6 - 2 = \underline{\hspace{1.5cm}}$$

2

Whole
○ ○ ○ ● ●
Part	Part
● ● ●	

$$5 - 3 = \underline{\hspace{1.5cm}}$$

3
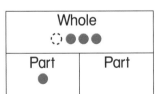

Whole
○ ● ● ●
Part	Part
●	

$$4 - 1 = \underline{\hspace{1.5cm}}$$

4
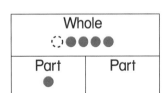

Whole
○ ● ● ● ●
Part	Part
●	

$$5 - 1 = \underline{\hspace{1.5cm}}$$

5
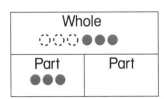

Whole
○ ○ ○ ● ● ●
Part	Part
● ● ●	

$$6 - 3 = \underline{\hspace{1.5cm}}$$

6

Whole
○ ○ ○ ○ ●
Part	Part
● ● ● ●	

$$5 - 4 = \underline{\hspace{1.5cm}}$$

Name _____ Date _____

75   **Draw how many you start with.**
Cross out the ones you subtract.
Write how many are left.

1

6 – 4 = ___2___

2

5 – 2 = _____

3

4 – 3 = _____

4

6 – 3 = _____

5

6 – 1 = _____

6

5 – 3 = _____

Math to Learn

Name _____ Date _____

$$6 - 2 = 4$$

---

76 **Count back to find the differences.**

1 7 − 1 = ___   **2** 5 − 2 = ___   **3** 6 − 2 = ___

4 9 − 1 = ___   **5** 8 − 2 = ___   **6** 4 − 1 = ___

7 6 − 1 = ___   **8** 7 − 2 = ___   **9** 5 − 1 = ___

10 8 − 1 = ___   **11** 9 − 2 = ___   **12** 10 − 1 = ___

13 10 − 2 = ___   **14** 3 − 1 = ___   **15** 11 − 2 = ___

16 8 − 3 = ___   **17** 10 − 3 = ___   **18** 9 − 3 = ___

Math to Learn

Name _____ Date _____

77

Count up from the number you subtract. Use this number line to help you.

0 1 2 3 4 5 6 7 8 9 10 11 12

Write the difference.

1 7 − 5 = ___   **2** 9 − 7 = ___   **3** 10 − 9 = ___

4 6 − 5 = ___   **5** 8 − 6 = ___   **6** 11 − 8 = ___

7 12 − 9 = ___   **8** 7 − 6 = ___   **9** 8 − 5 = ___

10 8 − 7 = ___   **11** 9 − 6 = ___   **12** 10 − 8 = ___

13 11 − 9 = ___   **14** 10 − 7 = ___   **15** 11 − 7 = ___

Name _____ Date _____

78–79   **Subtract.**

1   8 – 0 = ____   **2**   8 – 1 = ____   **3**   8 – 2 = ____

4   5 – 0 = ____   **5**   5 – 1 = ____   **6**   5 – 2 = ____

7   8 – 0 = ____   **8**   4 – 4 = ____   **9**   7 – 1 = ____

10   6 – 2 = ____   **11**   10 – 0 = ____   **12**   11 – 2 = ____

13   9 – 9 = ____   **14**   8 – 1 = ____   **15**   8 – 8 = ____

16   7 – 0 = ____   **17**   9 – 1 = ____   **18**   10 – 2 = ____

19   8 – 2 = ____   **20**   10 – 1 = ____   **21**   9 – 9 = ____

Write About Math

22   What happens when you subtract a number from itself?

_____

_____

Math to Learn

Name _____ Date _____

You can line up groups to compare.

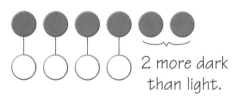

2 more dark than light.

$$6 - 4 = 2$$

There are 2 more dark counters than light counters.

80–81 **Find the difference.**

1

$$5 - 3 = \underline{\hspace{1cm}}$$

2

$$8 - 5 = \underline{\hspace{1cm}}$$

3

$$7 - 4 = \underline{\hspace{1cm}}$$

4

$$4 - 3 = \underline{\hspace{1cm}}$$

5 $9 - 5 = \underline{\hspace{0.5cm}}$ **6** $10 - 6 = \underline{\hspace{0.5cm}}$ **7** $12 - 8 = \underline{\hspace{0.5cm}}$

8 $11 - 5 = \underline{\hspace{0.5cm}}$ **9** $8 - 4 = \underline{\hspace{0.5cm}}$ **10** $10 - 5 = \underline{\hspace{0.5cm}}$

11 $12 - 5 = \underline{\hspace{0.5cm}}$ **12** $9 - 4 = \underline{\hspace{0.5cm}}$ **13** $11 - 6 = \underline{\hspace{0.5cm}}$

Name _____   Date _____

72–81   **Write the differences.**
Cross out the facts you know.
Keep track of facts you need to study.

Subtract 1	Subtract 2	Subtract 3	Subtract 4
$1 - 1 =$ ___	$2 - 2 =$ ___	$3 - 3 =$ ___	$4 - 4 =$ ___
$2 - 1 =$ ___	$3 - 2 =$ ___	$4 - 3 =$ ___	$5 - 4 =$ ___
$3 - 1 =$ ___	$4 - 2 =$ ___	$5 - 3 =$ ___	$6 - 4 =$ ___
$4 - 1 =$ ___	$5 - 2 =$ ___	$6 - 3 =$ ___	$7 - 4 =$ ___
$5 - 1 =$ ___	$6 - 2 =$ ___	$7 - 3 =$ ___	$8 - 4 =$ ___
$6 - 1 =$ ___	$7 - 2 =$ ___	$8 - 3 =$ ___	$9 - 4 =$ ___
$7 - 1 =$ ___	$8 - 2 =$ ___	$9 - 3 =$ ___	$10 - 4 =$ ___
$8 - 1 =$ ___	$9 - 2 =$ ___	$10 - 3 =$ ___	$11 - 4 =$ ___
$9 - 1 =$ ___	$10 - 2 =$ ___	$11 - 3 =$ ___	$12 - 4 =$ ___
$10 - 1 =$ ___	$11 - 2 =$ ___	$12 - 3 =$ ___	$13 - 4 =$ ___

Name _____ Date _____

72–81 **Write the differences.**
Cross out the facts you know.
Keep track of facts you need to study.

Subtract 5	Subtract 6	Subtract 7	Subtract 8
5 – 5 = ___	6 – 6 = ___	7 – 7 = ___	8 – 8 = ___
6 – 5 = ___	7 – 6 = ___	8 – 7 = ___	9 – 8 = ___
7 – 5 = ___	8 – 6 = ___	9 – 7 = ___	10 – 8 = ___
8 – 5 = ___	9 – 6 = ___	10 – 7 = ___	11 – 8 = ___
9 – 5 = ___	10 – 6 = ___	11 – 7 = ___	12 – 8 = ___
10 – 5 = ___	11 – 6 = ___	12 – 7 = ___	13 – 8 = ___
11 – 5 = ___	12 – 6 = ___	13 – 7 = ___	14 – 8 = ___
12 – 5 = ___	13 – 6 = ___	14 – 7 = ___	15 – 8 = ___
13 – 5 = ___	14 – 6 = ___	15 – 7 = ___	16 – 8 = ___
14 – 5 = ___	15 – 6 = ___	16 – 7 = ___	17 – 8 = ___

Name _____ Date _____

Subtraction

Write how many in all.
Write how many go away.
Write how many are left.

1 _____ − _____ = _____
are left

2  _____ − _____ = _____
are left

Draw how many you start with.
Cross out the ones you subtract.
Write how many are left.

3

$6 - 2 =$ _____

4

$5 - 4 =$ _____

Write the difference.

5 $5 - 2 =$ ____   **6** $6 - 3 =$ ____   **7** $9 - 0 =$ ____

8 $7 - 5 =$ ____   **9** $8 - 3 =$ ____   **10** $7 - 4 =$ ____

Name _____ Date _____

Subtraction

Fill in the ◯ next to the correct answer.

What is the difference?

1 9 − 3 = _____

(A) 3   (B) 5

(C) 6   (D) 7

2 10 − 4 = _____

(A) 5   (B) 6

(C) 4   (D) 8

3 11 − 2 = _____

(A) 6   (B) 7

(C) 8   (D) 9

4 7 − 0 = _____

(A) 7   (B) 1

(C) 0   (D) 6

5 8 − 5 = _____

(A) 2   (B) 3

(C) 4   (D) 5

6

$$\begin{array}{r} 10 \\ -\ 7 \\ \hline \end{array}$$

(A) 7

(B) 4

(C) 2

(D) 3

Math to Learn

PRACTICE ANSWERS
Page 60
1. $5 - 3 = 2$ 2. $6 - 4 = 2$
3. $6 - 3 = 3$ 4. $3 - 1 = 2$
5. $4 - 3 = 1$ 6. $5 - 3 = 2$

Page 61
1. 4   2. 2   3. 3
4. 4   5. 3   6. 1

Page 62
1. ⊘ ⊘ ○   2
   ⊘ ⊘ ○
2. ⊘ ○ ○   3
   ⊘ ○
3. ⊘ ⊘   1
   ⊘ ○
4. ⊘ ⊘ ○   3
   ⊘ ○ ○
5. ⊘ ○ ○   5
   ○ ○ ○
6. ⊘ ⊘ ○   2
   ⊘ ○

Page 63
1. 6   2. 3   3. 4
4. 8   5. 6   6. 3
7. 5   8. 5   9. 4
10. 7   11. 7   12. 9
13. 8   14. 2   15. 9
16. 5   17. 7   18. 6

Page 64
1. 2   2. 2   3. 1
4. 1   5. 2   6. 3
7. 3   8. 1   9. 3
10. 1   11. 3   12. 2
13. 2   14. 3   15. 4

Page 65
1. 8   2. 7   3. 6
4. 5   5. 4   6. 3
7. 8   8. 0   9. 6
10. 4   11. 10   12. 9
13. 0   14. 7   15. 0
16. 7   17. 8   18. 8
19. 6   20. 9   21. 0
22. You get zero.

Page 65
1. 8   2. 7   3. 6
4. 5   5. 4   6. 3
7. 8   8. 0   9. 6
10. 4   11. 10   12. 9
13. 0   14. 7   15. 0
16. 7   17. 8   18. 8
19. 6   20. 9   21. 0
22. When you subtract a number from itself, you get zero.

Page 66
1. 2   2. 3
3. 3   4. 1
5. 4   6. 4   7. 4
8. 6   9. 4   10. 5
11. 7   12. 5   13. 5

Page 67

Subtract 1	Subtract 2	Subtract 3	Subtract 4
$1 - 1 = 0$	$2 - 2 = 0$	$3 - 3 = 0$	$4 - 4 = 0$
$2 - 1 = 1$	$3 - 2 = 1$	$4 - 3 = 1$	$5 - 4 = 1$
$3 - 1 = 2$	$4 - 2 = 2$	$5 - 3 = 2$	$6 - 4 = 2$
$4 - 1 = 3$	$5 - 2 = 3$	$6 - 3 = 3$	$7 - 4 = 3$
$5 - 1 = 4$	$6 - 2 = 4$	$7 - 3 = 4$	$8 - 4 = 4$
$6 - 1 = 5$	$7 - 2 = 5$	$8 - 3 = 5$	$9 - 4 = 5$
$7 - 1 = 6$	$8 - 2 = 6$	$9 - 3 = 6$	$10 - 4 = 6$
$8 - 1 = 7$	$9 - 2 = 7$	$10 - 3 = 7$	$11 - 4 = 7$
$9 - 1 = 8$	$10 - 2 = 8$	$11 - 3 = 8$	$12 - 4 = 8$
$10 - 1 = 9$	$11 - 2 = 9$	$12 - 3 = 9$	$13 - 4 = 9$

Page 68

Subtract 5	Subtract 6	Subtract 7	Subtract 8
$5 - 5 = 0$	$6 - 6 = 0$	$7 - 7 = 0$	$8 - 8 = 0$
$6 - 5 = 1$	$7 - 6 = 1$	$8 - 7 = 1$	$9 - 8 = 1$
$7 - 5 = 2$	$8 - 6 = 2$	$9 - 7 = 2$	$10 - 8 = 2$
$8 - 5 = 3$	$9 - 6 = 3$	$10 - 7 = 3$	$11 - 8 = 3$
$9 - 5 = 4$	$10 - 6 = 4$	$11 - 7 = 4$	$12 - 8 = 4$
$10 - 5 = 5$	$11 - 6 = 5$	$12 - 7 = 5$	$13 - 8 = 5$
$11 - 5 = 6$	$12 - 6 = 6$	$13 - 7 = 6$	$14 - 8 = 6$
$12 - 5 = 7$	$13 - 6 = 7$	$14 - 7 = 7$	$15 - 8 = 7$
$13 - 5 = 8$	$14 - 6 = 8$	$15 - 7 = 8$	$16 - 8 = 8$
$14 - 5 = 9$	$15 - 6 = 9$	$16 - 7 = 9$	$17 - 8 = 9$

TEST PREP ANSWERS
Page 69
1. $5 - 2 = 3$ 2. $7 - 4 = 3$
3. ⊘ ○ ○   4
   ⊘ ○ ○
4. ⊘ ⊘ ⊘   1
   ⊘ ○
5. 3   6. 3   7. 9
8. 2   9. 5   10. 3

Page 70
1. C
2. B
3. D
4. A
5. B
6. D

Name _____ Date _____

Relating Addition and Subtraction

Fact families share the same three numbers.

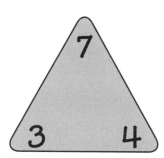

$3 + 4 = 7$ $7 - 4 = 3$

$4 + 3 = 7$ $7 - 3 = 4$

82–83 **Complete each fact family.**

1

$6 + 3 =$ _____ $9 - 3 =$ _____

$3 +$ ___ $=$ ___ $9 -$ ___ $=$ ___

2

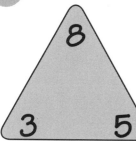

$3 + 5 =$ _____ $8 - 5 =$ _____

$5 +$ ___ $=$ ___ $8 -$ ___ $=$ ___

Name _____ Date _____

84–85 **You can use counters to find the missing part.**

Whole
○○○○○○

Part	Part
●●	●●●●

$$2 + 4 = 6$$
$$6 - 2 = 4$$

1
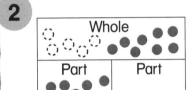

Whole

Part	Part

$$7 + \text{\_\_\_} = 12$$

$$12 - 7 = \text{\_\_\_}$$

2
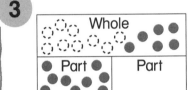

Whole

Part	Part

$$5 + \text{\_\_\_} = 13$$

$$13 - 5 = \text{\_\_\_}$$

3

Whole

Part	Part

$$9 + \text{\_\_\_} = 15$$

$$15 - 9 = \text{\_\_\_}$$

Write About Math

4 Tell how you can use addition to find the difference.

$$12 - 8 = \text{\_\_\_}$$

_____

_____

Name _____ Date _____

86 **Write the addition doubles fact.**
Use the addition fact to help you subtract.

1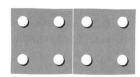

$\underline{4} + \underline{4} = \underline{8}$

$8 - 4 = \underline{\hspace{1cm}}$

2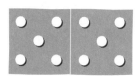

$\underline{\hspace{1cm}} + \underline{\hspace{1cm}} = \underline{\hspace{1cm}}$

$10 - 5 = \underline{\hspace{1cm}}$

3

$\underline{\hspace{1cm}} + \underline{\hspace{1cm}} = \underline{\hspace{1cm}}$

$12 - 6 = \underline{\hspace{1cm}}$

4

$\underline{\hspace{1cm}} + \underline{\hspace{1cm}} = \underline{\hspace{1cm}}$

$14 - 7 = \underline{\hspace{1cm}}$

5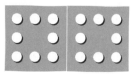

$\underline{\hspace{1cm}} + \underline{\hspace{1cm}} = \underline{\hspace{1cm}}$

$16 - 8 = \underline{\hspace{1cm}}$

6

$\underline{\hspace{1cm}} + \underline{\hspace{1cm}} = \underline{\hspace{1cm}}$

$18 - 9 = \underline{\hspace{1cm}}$

Name _____ Date _____

87 Write the addition facts.
Use the addition facts to help you subtract.

1

$\underline{9} + \underline{1} = \underline{10}$　　　$\underline{1} + \underline{9} = \underline{10}$

$10 - 1 = \underline{9}$　　　$10 - 9 = \underline{1}$

2

$\underline{\quad} + \underline{\quad} = 10$　　　$\underline{\quad} + \underline{\quad} = 10$

$10 - 2 = \underline{\quad}$　　　$10 - 8 = \underline{\quad}$

3

$\underline{\quad} + \underline{\quad} = 10$　　　$\underline{\quad} + \underline{\quad} = 10$

$10 - 3 = \underline{\quad}$　　　$10 - 7 = \underline{\quad}$

4

$\underline{\quad} + \underline{\quad} = 10$　　　$\underline{\quad} + \underline{\quad} = 10$

$10 - 4 = \underline{\quad}$　　　$10 - 6 = \underline{\quad}$

Math to Learn

Name _____ Date _____

88–89 Complete the addition table.

1

+	1	2	3	4	5	6	7	8
1								
2								
3						9		
4								
5								
6								

Use the addition table to subtract.

2 9 – 3 = ____   **3** 9 – 6 = ____   **4** 10 – 4 = ____

5 11 – 7 = ____   **6** 13 – 7 = ____   **7** 9 – 3 = ____

8 14 – 6 = ____   **9** 8 – 4 = ____   **10** 12 – 5 = ____

Name _____ Date _____

77 **Find each sum or difference.**

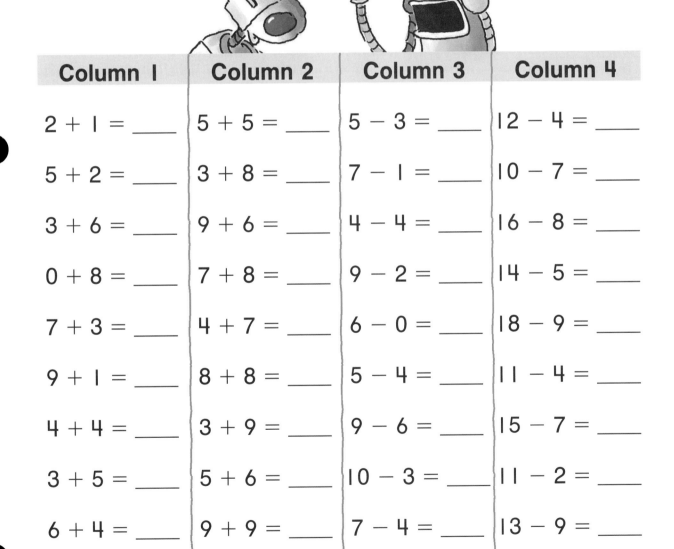

Column 1	Column 2	Column 3	Column 4
2 + 1 = ____	5 + 5 = ____	5 − 3 = ____	12 − 4 = ____
5 + 2 = ____	3 + 8 = ____	7 − 1 = ____	10 − 7 = ____
3 + 6 = ____	9 + 6 = ____	4 − 4 = ____	16 − 8 = ____
0 + 8 = ____	7 + 8 = ____	9 − 2 = ____	14 − 5 = ____
7 + 3 = ____	4 + 7 = ____	6 − 0 = ____	18 − 9 = ____
9 + 1 = ____	8 + 8 = ____	5 − 4 = ____	11 − 4 = ____
4 + 4 = ____	3 + 9 = ____	9 − 6 = ____	15 − 7 = ____
3 + 5 = ____	5 + 6 = ____	10 − 3 = ____	11 − 2 = ____
6 + 4 = ____	9 + 9 = ____	7 − 4 = ____	13 − 9 = ____
1 + 8 = ____	7 + 5 = ____	8 − 5 = ____	17 − 8 = ____

Name _____ Date _____

Relating Addition and Subtraction

Complete each fact family.

1

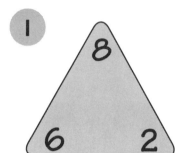

$6 + 2 =$ _____ $8 - 2 =$ _____

$2 +$ _____ $=$ _____ $8 -$ _____ $=$ _____

2

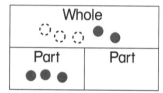

$3 +$ _____ $= 5$

$5 - 3 =$ _____

3

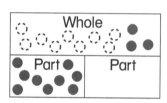

$9 +$ _____ $= 12$

$12 - 9 =$ _____

4

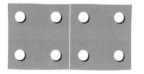

_4_ $+$ _4_ $=$ _8_

$8 - 4 =$ _____

5

_____ $+$ _____ $=$ _____

$14 - 7 =$ _____

Math to Learn

PRACTICE ANSWERS
Page 72

1. $6 + 3 = \underline{9}$ $9 - 3 = \underline{6}$
   $3 + \underline{6} = 9$ $9 - \underline{6} = \underline{3}$
2. $3 + 5 = \underline{8}$ $8 - 5 = \underline{3}$
   $5 + \underline{3} = \underline{8}$ $8 - \underline{3} = \underline{5}$

Page 73

1. 5, 5   2. 8, 8   3. 6, 6
4. Responses will vary. Possible response: If you know $8 + 4 = 12$, you know that $12 - 8 = 4$.

Page 74

1. $4 + 4 = 8, 4$
2. $5 + 5 = 10, 5$
3. $6 + 6 = 12, 6$
4. $7 + 7 = 14, 7$
5. $8 + 8 = 16, 8$
6. $9 + 9 = 18, 9$

Page 75

1. $9 + 1 = 10,$
   $1 + 9 = 10, 9, 1$
2. $8 + 2 = 10,$
   $2 + 8 = 10, 8, 2$
3. $7 + 3 = 10,$
   $3 + 7 = 10, 7, 3$
4. $6 + 4 = 10,$
   $4 + 6 = 10, 6, 4$

Page 76

1.

+	1	2	3	4	5	6	7	8
1	2	3	4	5	6	7	8	9
2	3	4	5	6	7	8	9	10
3	4	5	6	7	8	9	10	11
4	5	6	7	8	9	10	11	12
5	6	7	8	9	10	11	12	13
6	7	8	9	10	11	12	13	14

2. 6   3. 3   4. 6
5. 4   6. 6   7. 6
8. 8   9. 4   10. 7

Page 77

Column 1	Column 2	Column 3	Column 4
$2 + 1 = \underline{3}$	$5 + 5 = \underline{10}$	$5 - 3 = 2$	$12 - 4 = 8$
$5 + 2 = \underline{7}$	$3 + 8 = \underline{11}$	$7 - 1 = \underline{6}$	$10 - 7 = \underline{3}$
$3 + 6 = \underline{9}$	$9 + 6 = \underline{15}$	$4 - 4 = \underline{0}$	$16 - 8 = \underline{8}$
$0 + 8 = \underline{8}$	$7 + 8 = \underline{15}$	$9 - 2 = \underline{7}$	$14 - 5 = \underline{9}$
$7 + 3 = \underline{10}$	$4 + 7 = \underline{11}$	$6 - 0 = \underline{6}$	$18 - 9 = \underline{9}$
$9 + 1 = \underline{10}$	$8 + 8 = \underline{16}$	$5 - 4 = \underline{1}$	$11 - 4 = \underline{7}$
$4 + 4 = \underline{8}$	$3 + 9 = \underline{12}$	$9 - 6 = 3$	$15 - 7 = 8$
$3 + 5 = \underline{8}$	$5 + 6 = \underline{11}$	$10 - 3 = \underline{7}$	$11 - 2 = \underline{9}$
$6 + 4 = \underline{10}$	$9 + 9 = \underline{18}$	$7 - 4 = \underline{3}$	$13 - 9 = \underline{4}$
$1 + 8 = \underline{9}$	$7 + 5 = \underline{12}$	$8 - 5 = \underline{3}$	$17 - 8 = \underline{9}$

TEST PREP ANSWERS
Page 78

1. $6 + 2 = \underline{8}$ $8 - 2 = \underline{6}$
   $2 + \underline{6} = \underline{8}$ $8 - \underline{6} = \underline{2}$
2. 2, 2   3. 3, 3
4. $4 + 4 = 8, 4$
5. $7 + 7 = 14, 7$

Bean Bag Toss

OBJECTIVES
- Use three addends to find sums through 15
- To make an organized list

MATERIALS
- pencil and paper

TIME
- 20–30 minutes

TEACHER NOTES

- Read the task to the students.

- Explain that when a student throws three beanbags, each goes through a hole.

- Point out that it is possible that all three bean bags go through the same hole.

- Ask questions such as:

   What are three different numbers the bean bags might go through? What would the score be?

   What would the score be if all three bean bags went through the hole marked 3? (9)

   How can you find all possible scores?

EXTENSIONS

- Have students design a different bean bag board (on paper) and choose different numbers for each hole. Then have them repeat the activity using their own boards.

- Have children write about how they organized their data.

ANSWERS

All possible scores are shown. Ways to make the scores may differ.

Score	Way to make
15	5 + 5 + 5
6	2 + 2 + 2
7	2 + 2 + 3
8	2 + 2 + 4
9	2 + 3 + 4
10	4 + 4 + 2
11	3 + 3 + 5
12	5 + 5 + 2
13	5 + 5 + 3
14	5 + 5 + 4

You may wish to use this **scoring rubric** to assess students' work.

3 points	• Student develops and executes a plan to make a list of all possible scores. • Student writes the 10 possible scores. • Student writes a correct way to make each score.
2 points	• Student writes at least 6 possible scores. • Student writes a correct way to make at least 6 scores.
1 point	• Student writes fewer than 6 possible scores. • Student writes 6 possible scores but is unable to write a correct way to make each score.

Name _____ Date _____

Bean Bag Toss

Look at the Bean Bag board below. You throw 3 bean bags. Each goes through a hole.

- What is the highest score you can get?

- What is the lowest score you can get?

- List all the possible scores. For each different score, list one way to make that score.

HANDBOOK
HELP

Addition
  pages 54–71
Make a List
  pages 280–281

highest score

lowest score

Score	Way to make

Name _____ Date _____

Multiplication

Sometimes you have equal groups.
Then you can add or multiply to find the total.

3 groups of 2

$3 \times 2 = 6$

2   +   2   +   2   = 6

92–97   **Draw to show equal groups.**
Write the product.

1

4 groups of 2

$4 \times 2 = $ _____

2

2 groups of 3

$2 \times 3 = $ _____

3

2 groups of 5

$2 \times 5 = $ _____

4

3 groups of 4

$3 \times 4 = $ _____

Name _____ Date _____

98–107 **Draw circles in an array to show the multiplication fact. Write the product.**

1

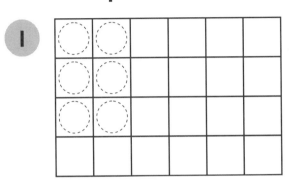

$$3 \times 2 = \underline{\hspace{1cm}}$$
↑   ↑   ↑

rows   in each   in all
      row

2

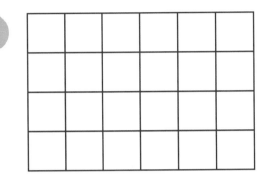

$$4 \times 5 = \underline{\hspace{1cm}}$$
↑   ↑   ↑

rows   in each   in all
      row

Write About Math

3 Write a story about $3 \times 4 = 12$.
Draw a picture about your story.

_____

_____

_____

_____

Name _____ Date _____

Multiplication

Fill in the ⬭ next to the correct answer.

Which number sentence matches the picture?

1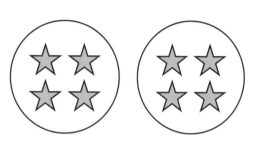

Ⓐ $2 + 4 = 6$

Ⓑ $2 \times 4 = 8$

Ⓒ $4 \times 4 = 16$

2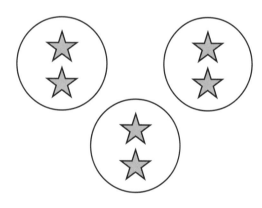

Ⓐ $3 \times 2 = 6$

Ⓑ $3 + 2 = 5$

Ⓒ $2 \times 2 = 4$

3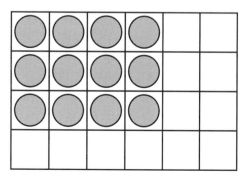

Ⓐ $3 \times 3 = 9$

Ⓑ $3 + 4 = 7$

Ⓒ $3 \times 4 = 12$

Math to Learn

PRACTICE ANSWERS
Page 82

1.

$4 \times 2 = \underline{8}$

2.

$2 \times 3 = \underline{6}$

3.

$2 \times 5 = \underline{10}$

4.

$3 \times 4 = \underline{12}$

Page 83

1.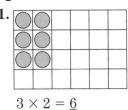

$3 \times 2 = \underline{6}$

2.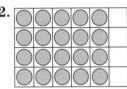

$4 \times 5 = \underline{20}$

3. Responses will vary. Sample response: There are 3 leaves. Each leaf has 4 bugs on it. There are 12 bugs in all.

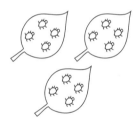

TEST PREP ANSWERS
Page 84

1. B
2. A
3. C

Name _____ Date _____

Division

108–109 **Use counters and the two boxes below.**

1 Share 6 counters evenly. How many in each box?

$6 \div 2 =$ _____

2 Share 10 counters evenly. How many in each box?

$10 \div 2 =$ _____

Use counters and the three boxes below.

3 Share 6 counters evenly. How many in each box?

$6 \div 3 =$ _____

4 Share 12 counters evenly. How many in each box?

$12 \div 3 =$ _____

Name _____ Date _____

110-111 **Circle the number in each group.**
Write how many groups.

 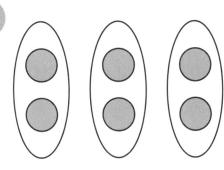

2 in each group

_3_ groups

$6 \div 2 = \underline{3}$

 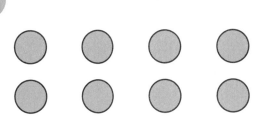

4 in each group

_____ groups

$8 \div 4 = \underline{}$

3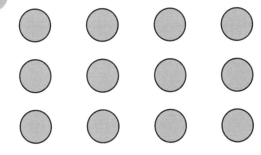

4 in each group

_____ groups

$12 \div 4 = \underline{}$

4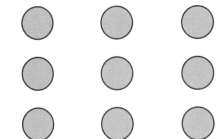

3 in each group

_____ groups

$9 \div 3 = \underline{}$

Name _____ Date _____

Division

Fill in the next to the correct answer.

1

(A) 2   (B) 8

(C) 4   (D) 6

$8 \div 2 =$ _____

2

(A) 8   (B) 3

(C) 9   (D) 4

$12 \div 4 =$ _____

3

(A) 5   (B) 4

(C) 6   (D) 3

$6 \div 2 =$ _____

PRACTICE ANSWERS
Page 86

1. 3
2. 5
3. 2
4. 4

Page 87

Students may circle the dots using different arrangements. Accept different ways of circling as long as students circle the appropriate number of dots, without circling any dot more than once. Sample:

1. 3, 3

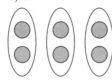

2. 2, 2

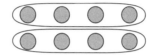

3. 3, 3

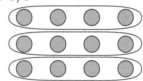

4. 3, 3

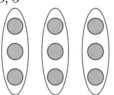

TEST PREP ANSWERS
Page 88

1. C
2. B
3. D

How Many Rectangles?

TIME
• 20–30 minutes

OBJECTIVES
• Use rectangles as array models for multiplication
• Use turn-around facts in multiplication (Order Property of Multiplication)
• Write multiplication sentences

MATERIALS
• grid paper
• scissors
• tape

TEACHER NOTES
• Read the task to the students.
• Review how rectangles look.
• Ask questions such as:

Look at the two rectangles in the picture. How are they the same? (They are the same rectangle, but they are in different positions. One looks tall and thin. The other looks short and wide.)
What two multiplication sentences can you write for the two rectangles in the picture? ($2 \times 6 = 12$ and $6 \times 2 = 12$)
Can you make a square using 12 squares? (No.)

EXTENSIONS
• Have students use grid paper to make rectangles that are also squares. Have them write a multiplication sentence for each. (Possible number sentences: $1 \times 1 = 1$, $2 \times 2 = 4$, $3 \times 3 = 9$, $4 \times 4 = 16$) *Why can't you write two multiplication sentences for each square?* (The length and width are the same.)

• Have students repeat the activity from page 91 using a different number of small squares. Examples:
  15 squares (2 rectangles, 4 multiplication sentences: $3 \times 5 = 15$, $5 \times 3 = 15$, $1 \times 15 = 15$, and $15 \times 1 = 15$)

  7 squares (1 rectangle, 2 multiplication sentences: $1 \times 7 = 7$ and $7 \times 1 = 7$)

  24 squares (4 rectangles, 8 multiplication sentences: $1 \times 24 = 24$, $24 \times 1 = 24$, $2 \times 12 = 24$, $12 \times 2 = 24$, $3 \times 8 = 24$, $8 \times 3 = 24$, $4 \times 6 = 24$, $6 \times 4 = 24$)

ANSWERS

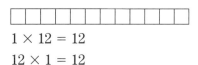

$1 \times 12 = 12$
$12 \times 1 = 12$

$2 \times 6 = 12$
$6 \times 2 = 12$

$3 \times 4 = 12$
$4 \times 3 = 12$

You may wish to use this **scoring rubric** to assess students' work.

3 points	• Student develops and executes a plan to find all possible rectangles. • Student makes 3 different rectangles using 12 squares. • Student correctly writes the 6 different multiplication sentences.
2 points	• Student makes at least 2 different rectangles using 12 squares. • Student correctly writes at least 4 different multiplication sentences.
1 point	• Student makes fewer than 2 different rectangles or writes fewer than 4 correct multiplication sentences.

Name _____ Date _____

How Many Rectangles?

We can get two multiplication sentences from one rectangle.

• Use grid paper to draw rectangles that have 12 small squares.

• Cut out the rectangles and tape them in the space below.

• Write two multiplication sentences for each rectangle.

• Use the back of this paper if you need more space.

Name _____ Date _____

Mental Math

114–116 **Add. Use mental math.**

1 3 + 4 = ___   **2** 30 + 40 = ___   **3** 35 + 40 = ___

4 2 + 6 = ___   **5** 20 + 60 = ___   **6** 20 + 62 = ___

7 4 + 1 = ___   **8** 40 + 10 = ___   **9** 40 + 16 = ___

117

10 29 + 4 = ___   **11** 45 + 3 = ___   **12** 37 + 5 = ___

13 50 + 6 = ___   **14** 89 + 5 = ___   **15** 65 + 5 = ___

16 46 + 5 = ___   **17** 72 + 6 = ___   **18** 32 + 9 = ___

118–119

19 4 + 2 = ___   **20** 400 + 200 = _____

21 428 + 200 = _____   **22** 300 + 163 = _____

116 Write About Math

23 Tell how you can use the hundred
chart to add 36 and 20.   _____

There is a hundred chart
on the inside back cover
of your handbook.

_____

Math to Learn

Name _____ Date _____

120–121 **Subtract. Use mental math.**

1 3 − 1 = _____   **2** 30 − 10 = _____

3 36 − 10 = _____   **4** 6 − 2 = _____

5 60 − 20 = _____   **6** 63 − 20 = _____

7 7 − 1 = _____   **8** 70 − 10 = _____

9 75 − 10 = _____   **10** 9 − 4 = _____

11 90 − 40 = _____   **12** 92 − 40 = _____

13 4 − 3 = _____   **14** 40 − 30 = _____

15 47 − 30 = _____   **16** 5 − 3 = _____

17 50 − 30 = _____   **18** 51 − 30 = _____

19 8 − 5 = _____   **20** 80 − 50 = _____

21 86 − 50 = _____   **22** 7 − 4 = _____

23 70 − 40 = _____   **24** 74 − 40 = _____

122–123

25 5 − 2 = _____   **26** 500 − 200 = _____

27 600 − 100 = _____   **28** 800 − 300 = _____

29 473 − 100 = _____   **30** 625 − 400 = _____

Math to Learn

Name _____   Date _____

Mental Math

Write each sum or difference.
Use mental math.

1 40 + 10 = _____   **2** 70 + 20 = _____

3 30 + 50 = _____   **4** 20 + 20 = _____

5 60 + 25 = _____   **6** 17 + 50 = _____

7 28 + 3 = _____   **8** 39 + 4 = _____

9 400 + 100 = _____   **10** 200 + 500 = _____

11 50 − 10 = _____   **12** 70 − 30 = _____

13 60 − 40 = _____   **14** 90 − 50 = _____

15 53 − 20 = _____   **16** 37 − 10 = _____

17 82 − 60 = _____   **18** 28 − 10 = _____

19 400 − 100 = _____   **20** 600 − 200 = _____

PRACTICE ANSWERS
Page 92

1. 7	**2.** 70	**3.** 75
4. 8	**5.** 80	**6.** 82
7. 5	**8.** 50	**9.** 56
10. 33	**11.** 48	**12.** 42
13. 56	**14.** 94	**15.** 70
16. 51	**17.** 78	**18.** 41
19. 6	**20.** 600	
21. 628	**22.** 463	

23. Answers will vary.
Sample answer: Find 36.
Go down two rows.
$36 + 20 = 56$

Page 93

1. 2	**2.** 20
3. 26	**4.** 4
5. 40	**6.** 43
7. 6	**8.** 60
9. 65	**10.** 5
11. 50	**12.** 52
13. 1	**14.** 10
15. 17	**16.** 2
17. 20	**18.** 21
19. 3	**20.** 30
21. 36	**22.** 3
23. 30	**24.** 34
25. 3	**26.** 300
27. 500	**28.** 500
29. 373	**30.** 225

TEST PREP ANSWERS
Page 94

1. 50	**2.** 90
3. 80	**4.** 40
5. 85	**6.** 67
7. 31	**8.** 43
9. 500	**10.** 700
11. 40	**12.** 40
13. 20	**14.** 40
15. 33	**16.** 27
17. 22	**18.** 18
19. 300	**20.** 400

Name _____ Date _____

Addition with Two-Digit and Three-Digit Numbers

124–125 **Write the sum.**

1

Tens	Ones
▬	▯▯
▬	▯▯▯

Tens	Ones
1	2
+1	3

2

Tens	Ones
▬▬	▯
	▯▯▯ ▯▯▯

Tens	Ones
2	1
+	6

3

Tens	Ones
▬▬▬▬	
▬▬	▯▯▯

Tens	Ones
4	0
+2	6

4

Tens	Ones
	▯▯ ▯▯
▬	▯▯▯ ▯▯

Tens	Ones
	4
+2	5

5

Tens	Ones
1	8
+2	4

6

Tens	Ones
1	0
+6	8

7

Tens	Ones
1	7
+8	0

8

Tens	Ones
2	6
+5	3

9

Tens	Ones
	4
+5	4

10

Tens	Ones
3	5
+1	4

11

Tens	Ones
	8
+7	1

12

Tens	Ones
2	5
+3	3

13

Tens	Ones
6	3
+2	6

14

Tens	Ones
5	2
+3	4

15

Tens	Ones
2	3
+	5

16

Tens	Ones
1	7
+8	0

Name _____ Date _____

23

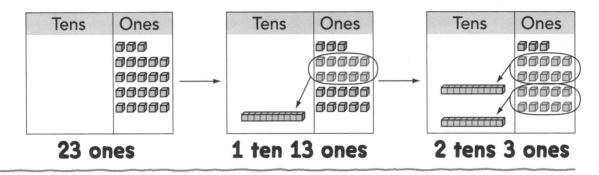

| 23 ones | 1 ten 13 ones | 2 tens 3 ones |

---

126   **Write ways to show each number.**

1   25

____0____ tens ___25___ ones

____1____ tens ___15___ ones

____2____ tens ___5___ ones

2   26

_____ tens _____ ones

_____ tens _____ ones

3   17

_____ tens _____ ones

_____ tens _____ ones

4   15

_____ tens _____ ones

_____ tens _____ ones

5   28

_____ tens _____ ones

_____ tens _____ ones

_____ tens _____ ones

6   29

_____ tens _____ ones

_____ tens _____ ones

_____ tens _____ ones

Name _____ Date _____

127–129   **Add.**

1

Tens	Ones
▭	▭▭▭▭▭ ▭▭▭
	▭▭▭▭

Tens	Ones
[1]	
1	8
+	4
2	2

2

Tens	Ones
▭ ▭ ▭	▭▭▭▭▭ ▭▭▭▭▭ ▭

Tens	Ones
□	
2	5
+1	6

3

Tens	Ones
□	
2	9
+1	4

4

Tens	Ones
□	
1	5
+2	5

5

Tens	Ones
□	
3	2
+	9

6

Tens	Ones
□	
1	4
+2	8

7

Tens	Ones
□	
1	6
+2	6

8

Tens	Ones
□	
	8
+3	2

9

Tens	Ones
□	
2	9
+1	1

10

Tens	Ones
□	
4	3
+1	7

Write About Math

11   Tell what mistake Rebecca made.
What should the answer be?

_____

_____

Rebecca

19
+43
52   X

Name _____ Date _____

127–129, 139

Do you need to regroup? Circle *yes* or *no*. Add.

Regroup only when necessary.

1

Tens	Ones
2	3
+	8

yes

no

2

Tens	Ones
1	4
+1	6

yes

no

3

Tens	Ones
2	4
+1	2

yes

no

4

Tens	Ones
3	8
+1	4

yes

no

5

Tens	Ones
4	5
+2	2

yes

no

6

Tens	Ones
2	7
+2	3

yes

no

Name _____ Date _____

127–129 **Add. Regroup if necessary.**

1
```
  43
+12
```

2
```
  58
+34
```

3
```
  19
+25
```

4
```
  26
+36
```

5
```
  41
+50
```

6
```
  22
+ 8
```

7
```
  71
+15
```

8
```
  34
+26
```

9
```
  40
+17
```

10
```
  40
+24
```

11
```
  19
+ 9
```

12
```
  56
+25
```

13
```
  82
+12
```

14
```
  47
+18
```

15
```
  32
+48
```

16
```
  37
+36
```

17
```
  60
+27
```

18
```
  28
+58
```

125, 127–129 **Line up addends by tens and ones. Add.**

19 26 + 32

20 55 + 18

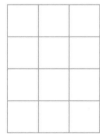

21 19 + 4

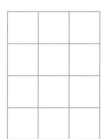

Name _____   Date _____

130–131   **Add.**

1

Hundreds	Tens	Ones

Hundreds	Tens	Ones
2	2	6
+ 1	4	0

132

2

Hundreds	Tens	Ones
4	2	6
+ 3	5	8

3

Hundreds	Tens	Ones
2	1	6
+ 5	3	4

4

Hundreds	Tens	Ones
4	0	9
+ 5	8	1

5

Hundreds	Tens	Ones
3	3	3
+ 2	0	8

6

Hundreds	Tens	Ones
5	2	5
+ 1	4	5

7

Hundreds	Tens	Ones
3	4	5
+ 1	1	8

133–137

8

Hundreds	Tens	Ones
3	2	6
+ 1	9	3

9

Hundreds	Tens	Ones
1	6	2
+ 2	5	6

10

Hundreds	Tens	Ones
	2	0
+ 4	8	7

11

Hundreds	Tens	Ones
	9	4
+	5	2

12

Hundreds	Tens	Ones
	3	5
+	9	1

13

Hundreds	Tens	Ones
	3	5
+	7	1

Math to Learn

Name _____ Date _____

Addition with Two-Digit and Three-Digit Numbers

Fill in the ⬭ next to the correct answer.
What is the sum?

1 24 + 3 = _____

  Ⓐ 26

  Ⓑ 27

  Ⓒ 37

2 46 + 6 = _____

  Ⓐ 42

  Ⓑ 54

  Ⓒ 52

3
53
+26

  Ⓐ 79

  Ⓑ 89

  Ⓒ 83

4
28
+34

  Ⓐ 512

  Ⓑ 52

  Ⓒ 62

5
40
+83

  Ⓐ 13

  Ⓑ 103

  Ⓒ 123

6
316
+258

  Ⓐ 574

  Ⓑ 674

  Ⓒ 5614

Name _____ Date _____

Addition with Two-Digit and Three-Digit Numbers

What is the sum?

1   25 + 3 = _____

2   8 + 26 = _____

3

Tens	Ones
3	4
+2	0

4

Tens	Ones
1	6
+2	6

5

Hundreds	Tens	Ones
1	2	4
+ 2	0	3

6   65
      +15

7   517
     +148

8   64
     +92

9   483
    +145

10   Samina used 35 blue beads and 45 purple beads to make a necklace. How many beads did she use?

_____ beads

PRACTICE ANSWERS
Page 96

1. 25   2. 27
3. 66   4. 29
5. 42
6. 78
7. 97
8. 79
9. 58
10. 49
11. 79
12. 58
13. 89
14. 86
15. 28
16. 97

Page 97

1. 25
   <u>0</u> tens <u>25</u> ones
   <u>1</u> tens <u>15</u> ones
   <u>2</u> tens <u>5</u> ones
2. 26
   0 tens 26 ones
   1 ten 16 ones
   2 tens 6 ones
3. 17
   0 tens 17 ones
   1 ten 7 ones
4. 15
   0 tens 15 ones
   1 ten 5 ones
5. 28
   0 tens 28 ones
   1 ten 18 ones
   2 tens 8 ones
6. 29
   0 tens 29 ones
   1 tens 19 ones
   2 tens 9 ones

Page 98

1. 22
2. 41
3. 43
4. 40
5. 41
6. 42
7. 42
8. 40
9. 40
10. 60
11. Answers may vary.
    Possible answer: She
    forgot to add the
    regrouped ten. The
    answer should be 62.

Page 99

1. yes; 31
2. yes; 30
3. no; 36
4. yes; 52
5. no; 67
6. yes; 50

Page 100

1. 55   2. 92   3. 44
4. 62   5. 91   6. 30
7. 86   8. 60   9. 57
10. 64   11. 28   12. 81
13. 94   14. 65   15. 80
16. 73   17. 87   18. 86
19. 58   20. 73   21. 23

Page 101

1. 366
2. 784   3. 750   4. 990
5. 541   6. 670   7. 463
8. 519   9. 418   10. 507
11. 146   12. 126   13. 106

TEST PREP ANSWERS
Page 102

1. B   2. C
3. A   4. C
5. C   6. A

Page 103

1. 28
2. 34
3. 54
4. 42
5. 327
6. 80
7. 665
8. 156
9. 628
10. 80

Name _____ Date _____

Subtraction with Two-Digit and Three-Digit Numbers

142–143 Write the difference.

1

Tens	Ones

Tens	Ones
2	5
− 1	3

2

Tens	Ones

Tens	Ones
1	7
−	6

3

Tens	Ones

Tens	Ones
4	3
− 1	2

4

Tens	Ones

Tens	Ones
2	5
−	5

5

Tens	Ones
5	8
−	6

6

Tens	Ones
7	3
− 2	3

7

Tens	Ones
6	5
− 4	0

8

Tens	Ones
9	5
− 5	3

9

Tens	Ones
4	1
− 3	1

10

Tens	Ones
7	9
−	5

11

Tens	Ones
8	4
− 6	3

12

Tens	Ones
4	8
− 2	4

13

Tens	Ones
8	8
− 3	6

14

Tens	Ones
4	5
− 2	1

15

Tens	Ones
3	2
− 1	2

16

Tens	Ones
6	7
− 4	4

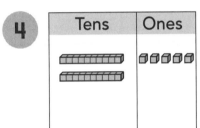

Math to Learn

Name _____ Date _____

Regroup 1 ten as 10 ones. Show how many now.

25

Tens	Ones
2	5

Tens	Ones
1	15
2	5

Tens	Ones
▭▭▭▭▭ ▭▭▭▭▭	◻◻◻◻◻

→

Tens	Ones
▭▭▭▭▭ ⬭▭▭▭▭▭	◻◻◻◻◻ ◻◻◻◻◻ ◻◻◻◻◻

2 tens 5 ones   **1 ten 15 ones**

---

144 ## Regroup 1 ten as 10 ones. Show how many now.

1
Tens	Ones
1	17
2	7

2
Tens	Ones
▢	▢
2	1

3
Tens	Ones
▢	▢
4	5

4
Tens	Ones
▢	▢
3	6

5
Tens	Ones
▢	▢
2	8

6
Tens	Ones
▢	▢
3	0

7
Tens	Ones
▢	▢
7	2

8
Tens	Ones
▢	▢
5	3

9
Tens	Ones
▢	▢
4	2

10
Tens	Ones
▢	▢
6	4

11
Tens	Ones
▢	▢
5	0

12
Tens	Ones
▢	▢
8	1

13
Tens	Ones
▢	▢
6	0

14
Tens	Ones
▢	▢
2	3

15
Tens	Ones
▢	▢
3	1

16
Tens	Ones
▢	▢
9	0

17
Tens	Ones
▢	▢
5	1

18
Tens	Ones
▢	▢
7	4

19
Tens	Ones
▢	▢
4	6

20
Tens	Ones
▢	▢
6	2

Name _____　Date _____

145–147　**Subtract.**

1

Tens	Ones
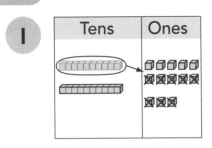

Tens	Ones
1	13
2	3̶
−	8

2

Tens	Ones
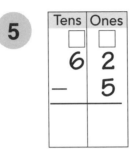

Tens	Ones
3	11
4̶	1̶
−	6

3

Tens	Ones
☐	☐
3	5
−	8

4

Tens	Ones
☐	☐
5	0
−	4

5

Tens	Ones
☐	☐
6	2
−	5

6

Tens	Ones
☐	☐
7	0
−	8

7

Tens	Ones
☐	☐
3	3
−	9

8

Tens	Ones
☐	☐
4	2
−	8

9

Tens	Ones
☐	☐
2	4
−	5

10

Tens	Ones
☐	☐
5	2
−	6

11

Tens	Ones
☐	☐
6	4
−	5

12

Tens	Ones
☐	☐
3	6
−	9

13

Tens	Ones
☐	☐
7	2
−	4

14

Tens	Ones
☐	☐
4	0
−	5

Name _____ Date _____

145–147 **Subtract.**

1

Tens	Ones
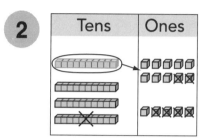

Tens	Ones
2	11
3	1
—	6

2

Tens	Ones
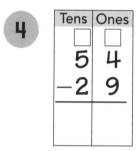

Tens	Ones
3	15
4	5
—1	7

3

Tens	Ones
☐	☐
4	2
−1	4

4

Tens	Ones
☐	☐
5	4
−2	9

5

Tens	Ones
☐	☐
3	2
−1	8

6

Tens	Ones
☐	☐
6	0
−2	5

7

Tens	Ones
☐	☐
4	1
−3	3

8

Tens	Ones
☐	☐
8	1
−2	7

Write About Math

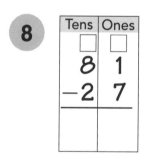

9 When you subtract, how do you know when to regroup tens as ones?

_____

_____

Name _____ Date _____

145–147 **Do you need to regroup?**
Circle *yes* or *no*. Subtract.

1

Tens	Ones
2	3
−	8

yes

no

2

Tens	Ones
5	4
−1	2

yes

no

3

Tens	Ones
3	4
−2	0

yes

no

4

Tens	Ones
6	0
−1	8

yes

no

5

Tens	Ones
4	1
−2	6

yes

no

6

Tens	Ones
3	7
−1	7

yes

no

Name _____   Date _____

142–147 ## Subtract. Regroup if necessary.

1   31
       −12

2   60
       −15

3   49
       −20

4   56
       −36

5   82
       −56

6   32
       − 8

7   44
       −17

8   35
       −14

9   70
       −30

10   51
        −29

11   44
        − 7

12   92
        −32

13   36
        −18

14   50
        −21

15   47
        −21

16   64
        −38

17   73
        −50

18   52
        −24

143 ## Line up addends by tens and ones. Subtract.

19   43 − 13

20   52 − 28

21   32 − 7

Name _____   Date _____

148–149   ## Subtract.

1

Hundreds	Tens	Ones

Hundreds	Tens	Ones
3	4	5
− 1	2	2

2

Hundreds	Tens	Ones
5	0	8
− 3	0	5

3

Hundreds	Tens	Ones
7	3	9
− 2	3	3

4

Hundreds	Tens	Ones
2	5	0
−	4	0

5

Hundreds	Tens	Ones
6	7	3
− 4	0	3

6

Hundreds	Tens	Ones
5	6	2
− 5	4	2

7

Hundreds	Tens	Ones
1	4	8
−	3	2

Math to Learn

Name _____ Date _____

150 ## Subtract.

1

Hundreds	Tens	Ones
4	6	1
− 1	4	8

2

Hundreds	Tens	Ones
2	8	4
− 1	0	6

3

Hundreds	Tens	Ones
3	5	0
−	2	8

154–155

4

Hundreds	Tens	Ones
3	2	8
− 1	8	3

5

Hundreds	Tens	Ones
6	4	9
− 2	5	7

6

Hundreds	Tens	Ones
4	1	6
−	5	5

Sometimes you need to regroup and sometimes you don't.

7

Hundreds	Tens	Ones
5	2	6
− 1	6	8

8

Hundreds	Tens	Ones
6	5	2
− 3	9	4

9

Hundreds	Tens	Ones
8	5	6
− 2	8	3

10

Hundreds	Tens	Ones
7	3	5
− 1	0	5

156–157 ## Subtract. Use addition to check your subtraction.

11

Hundreds	Tens	Ones
6	0	2
− 2	6	4

+ 2 6 4

Name _____   Date _____

Subtraction with Two-Digit and Three-Digit Numbers

Fill in the ◯ next to the correct answer.
What is the difference?

1   34 − 8 = _____

  Ⓐ 24

  Ⓑ 26

  Ⓒ 16

2   48 − 15 = _____

  Ⓐ 13

  Ⓑ 23

  Ⓒ 33

3   62
     −37

  Ⓐ 25

  Ⓑ 15

  Ⓒ 35

4   85
     −20

  Ⓐ 55

  Ⓑ 75

  Ⓒ 65

5   60
     −23

  Ⓐ 43

  Ⓑ 47

  Ⓒ 37

6   564
     −162

  Ⓐ 402

  Ⓑ 422

  Ⓒ 484

Math to Learn

Name _____ Date _____

Subtraction with Two-Digit and Three-Digit Numbers

What is the difference?

1 28 − 15 = _____

2 46 − 14 = _____

3

Tens	Ones
6	4
−2	0

4

Tens	Ones
5	4
−	9

5
70
−24

6
33
−13

7
465
−142

8
142
− 38

9
400
−270

10
515
−203

11 There are 156 students in the second grade. On Monday, 19 were absent. How many students were at school on Monday?

_____ students

PRACTICE ANSWERS
Page 105

1. 12
2. 11
3. 31
4. 20
5. 52
6. 50
7. 25
8. 42
9. 10
10. 74
11. 21
12. 24
13. 52
14. 24
15. 20
16. 23

Page 106

1.
Tens	Ones
1	17
2	7

2.
Tens	Ones
1	11
2	1

3.
Tens	Ones
3	15
4	5

4.
Tens	Ones
2	16
3	6

5.
Tens	Ones
1	18
2	8

6.
Tens	Ones
2	10
3	0

7.
Tens	Ones
6	12
7	2

8.
Tens	Ones
4	13
5	3

9.
Tens	Ones
3	12
4	2

10.
Tens	Ones
5	14
6	4

11.
Tens	Ones
4	10
5	0

12.
Tens	Ones
7	11
8	1

13.
Tens	Ones
5	10
6	0

14.
Tens	Ones
1	13
2	3

15.
Tens	Ones
2	11
3	1

16.
Tens	Ones
8	10
9	0

17.
Tens	Ones
4	11
5	1

18.
Tens	Ones
6	14
7	4

19.
Tens	Ones
3	16
4	6

20.
Tens	Ones
5	12
6	2

Page 107

1. 15
2. 35
3. 23
4. 46
5. 57
6. 62
7. 24
8. 34
9. 19
10. 46
11. 59
12. 27
13. 68
14. 35

Page 108

1. 25
2. 28
3. 28
4. 25
5. 14
6. 35
7. 8
8. 54
9. Answers may vary.
Possible answers: You
regroup when there are
not enough ones to
subtract. You regroup
when the bottom digit is
greater than the top
digit.

Page 109

1. yes; 15
2. no; 44
3. no; 24
4. yes; 42
5. yes; 15
6. no; 20

Page 110

1. 19
2. 45
3. 29
4. 20
5. 26
6. 24
7. 27
8. 21
9. 40
10. 22
11. 37
12. 60
13. 18
14. 29
15. 26
16. 26
17. 23
18. 28
19. 30
20. 24
21. 25

Page 111

1. 223
2. 203
3. 506
4. 210
5. 270
6. 20
7. 116

Page 112

1. 313
2. 178
3. 322
4. 145
5. 392
6. 361
7. 358
8. 258
9. 573
10. 630
11. 338 $338 + 264 = 602$

TEST PREP ANSWERS
Page 113

1. B
2. C
3. A
4. C
5. C
6. A

Page 114

1. 13
2. 32
3. 44
4. 45
5. 46
6. 20
7. 323
8. 104
9. 130
10. 312
11. 137

Name _____ Date _____

Estimating Sums and Differences

158 **Is the sum greater than 50? Circle _yes_ or _no_.**

1 $32 + 49$ yes no   **2** $17 + 6$ yes no

Estimate by rounding each addend to the nearest ten.

3 $31 + 47$ is about _____.   **4** $32 + 39$ is about _____.

5 $42 + 39$ is about _____.   **6** $48 + 37$ is about _____.

159 **Is the sum greater than 500? Circle _yes_ or _no_.**

7 $414 + 165$ yes no   **8** $246 + 107$ yes no

Estimate by rounding each addend to the nearest hundred.

9 $427 + 489$ is about _____.

10 $116 + 395$ is about _____.

Estimate by using front-end estimation.

11 $427 + 489$ is about _____.

12 $116 + 395$ is about _____.

Name _____ Date _____

160   **Is the difference greater than 50?**
Circle *yes* or *no*.

1   41 − 35   yes   no   **2**   78 − 13   yes   no

Estimate by rounding each number to the nearest ten.

3   61 − 47 is about _____.   **4**   86 − 34 is about _____.

5   59 − 36 is about _____.   **6**   48 − 23 is about _____.

161   **Is the difference greater than 500?**
Circle yes or no.

7   714 − 386   yes   no   **8**   786 − 104   yes   no

Estimate by rounding each number to the nearest hundred.

9   793 − 423 is about _____.

10   579 − 186 is about _____.

Estimate by using front-end estimation.

11   793 − 423 is about _____.

12   579 − 186 is about _____.

Name _____ Date _____

Estimating Sums and Differences

Fill in the ⬭ next to the correct answer.
Estimate by rounding each number to the nearest ten.

1 48 + 21 = _____

    A 70

    B 50

    C 30

2 41 + 13 = _____

    A 60

    B 20

    C 50

3 47 − 19 = _____

    A 10

    B 20

    C 30

4 92 − 38 = _____

    A 20

    B 50

    C 40

Estimate by rounding each number
to the nearest hundred.

5 592 + 107 = _____

    A 600

    B 700

    C 800

6 613 − 287 = _____

    A 500

    B 300

    C 200

PRACTICE ANSWERS
Page 116

1. yes
2. no
3. 80
4. 70
5. 80
6. 90
7. yes
8. no
9. 900
10. 500
11. 800
12. 400

Page 117

1. no
2. yes
3. 10
4. 60
5. 20
6. 30
7. no
8. yes
9. 400
10. 400
11. 300
12. 400

TEST PREP ANSWERS
Page 118

1. A
2. C
3. C
4. B
5. B
6. B

Magic Squares

OBJECTIVES
- Add two-digit numbers.
- Add three addends.
- Use subtraction to find a missing addend.
- Subtract two-digit numbers.

MATERIALS
- paper and pencil

TIME
- 25–35 minutes

TEACHER NOTES
- In a magic square, the sum of each row, column, and diagonal is the same. The sum is called the magic sum.

- Before giving students page 121, draw this 3 by 3 grid on the board.

	9	
7	5	
	1	8

- Point out the three rows, the three columns, and the two diagonals.

- Ask questions such as:

What numbers are in the middle row? (7 and 5)

What number is in the last column? (8)

What numbers are in the diagonal that begins here? (Point to the square in the upper left corner.) (5 and 8)

- Tell students that this square is called a "magic square." The sum of the numbers in any row, column, or diagonal is the same and is called the "magic sum." For this square, the magic sum is 15.

- Discuss ways to find the missing numbers in this magic square. (Use a row, column, or diagonal that has two numbers. Find the sum. Subtract the sum from 15.)

2	9	4
7	5	3
6	1	8

- Complete the magic square as a class.

EXTENSION
- Have students make up their own magic square using the numbers 22-30. The magic sum is 78.

23	30	25
28	26	24
27	22	29

ANSWERS
1.

11	18	13
16	14	12
15	10	17

2.

13	20	15
18	16	14
17	12	19

You may wish to use this **scoring rubric** to assess students' work.

3 points	• Student develops and executes a plan to correctly complete both magic squares.
2 points	• Student completes at least one of the two magic squares.
1 point	• Student is unable to complete either magic square.

Name _____ Date _____

Magic Squares

In a **magic square**, the sum of each row, column, and diagonal is the same. In this magic square, the sum is 15.

2	9	4
7	5	3
6	1	8

15 is called the **magic sum.**

Rows

2 + 9 + 4 = 15

7 + 5 + 3 = 15

6 + 1 + 8 = 15

Columns

2 + 7 + 6 = 15

9 + 5 + 1 = 15

4 + 3 + 8 = 15

Diagonals

2 + 5 + 8 = 15

4 + 5 + 6 = 15

Fill in the missing numbers in these magic squares.

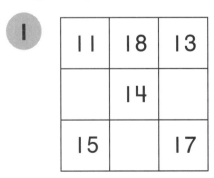

1

11	18	13
	14	
15		17

2

13		15
	16	
17		

Magic Sum is 42.   Magic Sum is 48.

Name _____ Date _____

Money

164–166   ## Skip count and count on to find the total.

1

10¢   20¢   30¢ ____   ____

[ ] total

2

____   ____   ____   ____   ____   ____

[ ] total

3

5¢   10¢   15¢ ____   ____

[ ] total

4

____   ____   ____   ____   ____   ____

[ ] total

Name _____ Date _____

167   **Skip count and count on to find the total.**

1

<u> 10¢ </u>   _____   _____   _____ | |

total

2

_____   _____   _____   _____ | |

total

3

<u> 5¢ </u>   _____   _____   _____ | |

total

4

_____   _____   _____   _____ | |

total

Math to Learn

Name _____ Date _____

168–169 **Skip count and count on to find the total.**

1

25¢ _____ _____

[ ] total

2

_____ _____ _____ _____ _____

[ ] total

3

_____ _____ _____ _____

[ ] total

4

_____ _____ _____ _____ _____

[ ] total

Name _____ Date _____

169–171   ## Skip count and count on to find the total.

1

25¢ ____ ____ ____ ____

[ ] total

2

____ ____ ____ ____ ____

[ ] total

3

____ ____ ____ ____ ____

[ ] total

4

____ ____ ____ ____ ____

[ ] total

© Great Source. Permission is granted to copy this page.

Math to Learn

Name _____ Date _____

172–175 **What is the total cost of the two toys?**
Show your work.

1

24¢

52¢

+ _____

2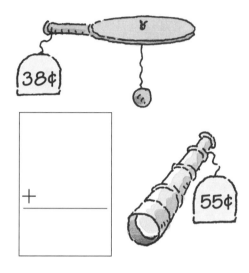

38¢

55¢

+ _____

3

$1.25

$2.50

+ _____

4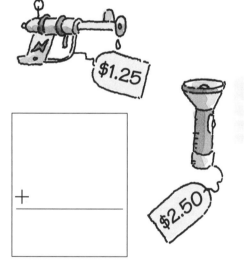

$2.66

$3.80

+ _____

Add.

5   34¢
     +42¢

6   55¢
     +25¢

7 $2.40
     +3.20

8 $1.75
     +2.49

Name _____ Date _____

176–179

1 Who has more money? _____

2 How much more money does _____ have?

_____

3 You buy a  38¢ .

You give the clerk .

How much change will the clerk give you? _____

4 You buy a 64¢ .

You give the clerk .

How much change will the clerk give you? _____

Name _____ Date _____

Money

Write the total value.

1   total

2   total

3    total

4   total

5   total

6   total

Name _____ Date _____

Money

Write the total value.

 1
[ ] total

 2 [ ] total

 3
[ ] total

4
[ ] total

5
[ ] total

6
[ ] total

Math to Learn

Name _____ Date _____

Money

Fill in the ◯ for the correct answer.

1 What is the total value?

(A) 30¢

(B) 35¢

(C) 40¢

2 What is the total value?

(A) 61¢

(B) 52¢

(C) 36¢

---

3 What is the total cost?

(A) 87¢   (B) 75¢   (C) 77¢

---

4 You buy a  42¢ . You give the clerk  .

How much change will the clerk give you?

(A) 18¢   (B) 8¢   (C) 92¢

---

5 $3.05   (A) $5.06
        +$2.41
                 (B) $6.46

                 (C) $5.46

6 $7.58   (A) $3.12
        −$3.46
                 (B) $4.12

                 (C) $4.98

Math to Learn

PRACTICE ANSWERS
Page 122

1. 10¢, 20¢, 30¢, 40¢, 50¢
   50¢

2. 10¢, 20¢, 30¢, 40¢, 50¢,
   60¢ 60¢

3. 5¢, 10¢, 15¢, 20¢, 25¢
   25¢

4. 5¢, 10¢, 15¢, 20¢, 25¢,
   30¢ 30¢

Page 123

1. 10¢, 20¢, 30¢, 31¢, 32¢
   32¢

2. 10¢, 20¢, 21¢, 22¢, 23¢
   23¢

3. 5¢, 10¢, 15¢, 20¢, 21¢
   21¢

4. 10¢, 15¢, 16¢, 17¢, 18¢
   18¢

Page 124

1. 25¢, 50¢, 75¢ 75¢

2. 25¢, 50¢, 75¢, $1.00,
   $1.25 $1.25

3. 25¢, 35¢, 45¢, 55¢ 55¢

4. 25¢, 50¢, 55¢, 60¢, 65¢
   65¢

Page 125

1. 25¢, 50¢, 75¢, 76¢, 77¢
   77¢

2. 25¢, 35¢, 45¢, 55¢, 60¢
   60¢

3. 10¢, 20¢, 30¢, 35¢, 36¢
   36¢

4. 25¢, 35¢, 40¢, 41¢, 42¢
   42¢

Page 126

1. 76¢
2. 93¢
3. $3.75
4. $6.46
5. 76¢
6. 80¢
7. $5.60
8. $4.24

Page 127

1. Nat
2. How much more money
   does Nat have? 5¢
3. 12¢
4. 11¢

TEST PREP ANSWERS
Page 128

1. 30¢
2. 20¢
3. 25¢
4. 21¢
5. 33¢
6. 28¢

Page 129

1. 50¢
2. 75¢
3. $1.25
4. 52¢
5. 46¢
6. 46¢

Page 130

1. C
2. C
3. A
4. B
5. C
6. B

Name _____ Date _____

Time

180–183   **What time is it?**

1   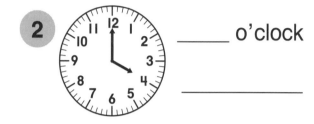 ___ o'clock
_9_
_9:00_

2   ___ o'clock
_____

3   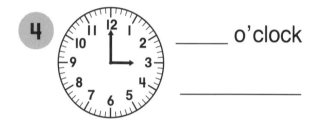 ___ o'clock

4   ___ o'clock
_____

5   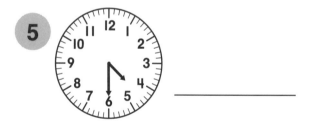 _____

6   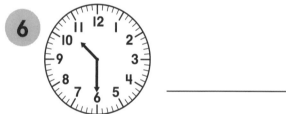 _____

7   _____

8    _____

9   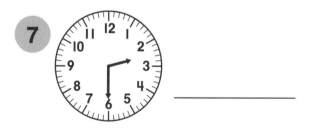 _____

10    _____

Name _____ Date _____

184–185 **What time is it?**

1

_____

2

3

4

_____

5

6

7

_____

8

9

10

_____

11

12

Name _____ Date _____

186 **What time is it?**

1

2

3

_____ _____ _____

187

4 It is 4:15. What time will it be in 10 minutes?

5 It is 10:30. What time will it be in a half hour?

_____ _____

188–189

6 The baby took a nap from 2 o'clock to 4 o'clock.

How long did the baby sleep? _____

7 The party will start at 5:30 P.M. and end at 8:00 P.M.

How long is the party? _____

Math to Learn

Name _____ Date _____

181

1 Estimate what number you can count to in one minute. Check your estimate.

_____   _____

my estimate   how far I really counted

2 How many minutes are in an hour? _____

3 How many hours are in a day? _____

190–191

Look at a calendar for this year.

4 What is the first day of this month? _____

5 What day of the week is the 15th day of this month?

_____

6 How many months are in a year? _____

7 Write the date you were born. Write the month, day, and year.

_____

Math to Learn

Name _____ Date _____

Time

Fill in the ⬭ for the correct answer.
What time does the clock show?

1

(A) 12 o'clock

(B) 4 o'clock

(C) 5 o'clock

2

(A) 12:00

(B) 9:00

(C) 3:00

3

(A) 2:30

(B) 6:30

(C) 3:30

4

(A) 3:00

(B) 3:05

(C) 3:01

5 What day of the week is March 10?

(A) Tuesday

(B) Wednesday

(C) Thursday

MARCH 2004						
Sun.	Mon.	Tues.	Wed.	Thurs.	Fri.	Sat.
	1	2	3	4	5	6
7	8	9	10	11	12	13
14	15	16	17	18	19	20
21	22	23	24	25	26	27
28	29	30	31			

PRACTICE ANSWERS
Page 132

1. 9 o'clock, 9:00
2. 4 o'clock, 4:00
3. 10 o'clock, 10:00
4. 3 o'clock, 3:00
5. 4:30
6. 10:30
7. 2:30
8. 11:00
9. 5:30
10. 12:30

Page 133

1. 9:05
2. 9:10
3. 9:15
4. 2:20
5. 2:25
6. 2:30
7. 5:35
8. 5:40
9. 5:45
10. 2:15
11. 4:50
12. 7:55

Page 134

1. 4:02
2. 7:21
3. 2:33
4. 4:25
5. 11:00
6. 2 hours
7. $2\frac{1}{2}$ hours

Page 135

1. Answers will vary. Perfectionists are especially reluctant to estimate. Encourage students to write their estimates before they find out how far they can actually count in one minute.
2. 60
3. 24
4.–5. Answers will vary according to the year and month.
6. 12
7. Answers will vary depending on students' birthdates. Accept various forms: August 31, 1997 or 8/31/97.

TEST PREP ANSWERS
Page 136

1. C
2. B
3. A
4. B
5. B

Different Ways to Share 9 Dimes

OBJECTIVES
- Add tens.
- Count money.
- Compare money amounts.
- Use a table to organize data to find different problem solutions.
- Use the problem-solving strategy guess, check, and revise.

MATERIALS
- paper and pencil

TIME
- 20–30 minutes

TEACHER NOTES
- Review values for 1 dime, 2 dimes, 3 dimes . . . 9 dimes (10¢, 20¢ 30¢, . . . 90¢).

- Ask questions such as:

  Who will get the least amount of money? (Tyler)

  What is the least amount of money Tyler could get? (10¢)

  Who gets the most money? (Eva)

  Is it possible that Eva gets exactly 10¢? (No.) *exactly 20¢?* (No, because Eva has more than Rosa and Rosa has more than Tyler.)

  Is it possible that Eva gets exactly 30¢? (No. If Eva gets 30¢, Rosa gets 20¢, and Tyler gets 10¢, and they do not have a total of 90¢)

- If the 90¢ total is too overwhelming, begin with a lesser amount such as 60¢. (For 60¢, there will only be one solution: Tyler: 10¢, Rosa: 20¢, and Eva: 30¢)

EXTENSIONS
Challenge students to show other ways the three children can share 90¢. Keep some of the rules the same (Tyler will get less money than Eva, Tyler will get less money than Rosa, and Rosa will get less money than Eva.) However, instead of dimes, students may use any number of quarters or nickels. Each child must get at least one coin, but no more than five coins.

Answers will vary. Sample answers:

Tyler	Rosa	Eva
5¢ (1 nickel)	10¢ (2 nickels)	75¢ (3 quarters)
10¢ (2 nickels)	15¢ (3 nickels)	65¢ (2 quarters 3 nickels)
15¢ (3 nickels)	20¢ (4 nickels)	55¢ (2 quarters 1 nickel)
15¢ (3 nickels)	25¢ (1 quarter)	50¢ (2 quarters)

ANSWERS

Tyler	Rosa	Eva
10¢	20¢	60¢
10¢	30¢	50¢
20¢	30¢	40¢

You may wish to use this **scoring rubric** to assess students' work.

3 points	• Student uses the least number of dimes (amounts of money) for Tyler and greatest number for Eva. • Student uses exactly 9 dimes (90¢) for each total. • Student completes the chart for 3 different ways to share 90¢.
2 points	• Student uses the least number of dimes (amounts of money) for Tyler and greatest number for Eva. • Student completes the chart for 1 or 2 different ways to share 90¢.
1 point	• Student sums do not total 90¢ or • Student does not use the least number of dimes (amounts of money) for Tyler and greatest number for Eva.

Name _____ Date _____

Different Ways to Share 9 Dimes

The three children will share 9 dimes,
but not equally!

• They will each get at least 10¢.

• Tyler will get less money than Eva.

• Tyler will get less money than Rosa.

• Rosa will get less money than Eva.

Show 3 different ways the children can share
the money.

Tyler	Rosa	Eva

Name _____ Date _____

Lines

194 **Use a word from the Word Bank to describe each.**

Word Bank
horizontal   vertical

1

_____

2

_____

3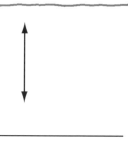

_____

4

_____

195 **Will these lines ever cross? Circle yes or no.**

5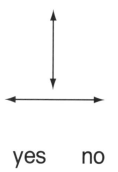

yes   no

6

yes   no

7

yes   no

Name _____ Date _____

Lines

Fill in the ◯ **for the correct answer.**

1   Which is a horizontal line?

(A)

(B)

(C)

2   Which is a vertical line?

(A)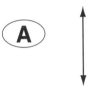

(B)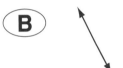

(C)

3   Which two lines will cross?

(A)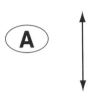

(B)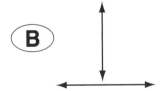

(C)

4   Which two lines will never cross?

(A)

(B)

(C)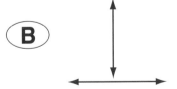

PRACTICE ANSWERS
Page 140

1. horizontal
2. vertical
3. vertical
4. horizontal
5. yes
6. no
7. yes

TEST PREP ANSWERS
Page 141

1. C
2. A
3. B
4. A

Name _____ Date _____

Plane Figures

196 Write the name of each shape.

Word Bank
circle   rectangle   triangle

1

_____

2

_____

3

_____

4

_____

5

_____

6

_____

197 Is the plane figure a closed figure?
Circle yes or no.

7

yes   no

8

yes   no

9

yes   no

How many sides?

10 triangle

_____

11 hexagon

_____

12 quadrilateral

_____

Name _____ Date _____

198–199　**Draw a line of symmetry through each figure.**

1

2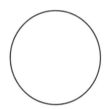

3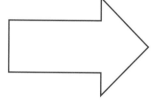

4

5 Finish drawing the shape to show symmetry.

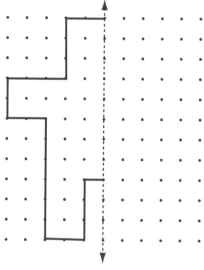

200–201　**Are the two figures congruent? Circle yes or no.**

6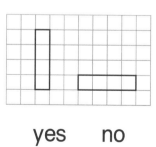

yes　　no

7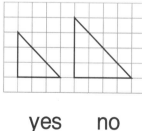

yes　　no

8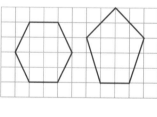

yes　　no

Name _____   Date _____

202–203   **Is each move a slide, flip, or turn?**
Circle the answer.

1
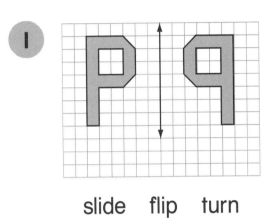
slide   flip   turn

2
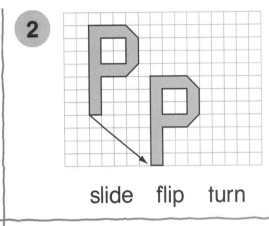
slide   flip   turn

3
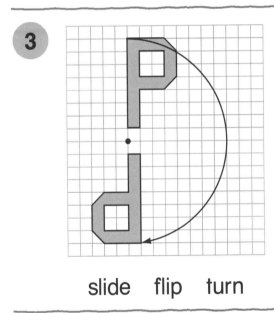
slide   flip   turn

4
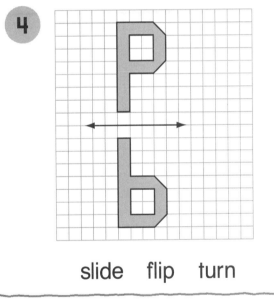
slide   flip   turn

5
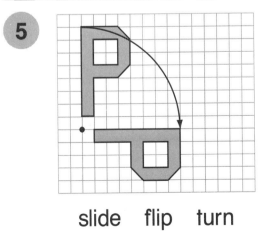
slide   flip   turn

6
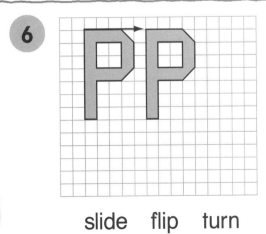
slide   flip   turn

Name _____ Date _____

Plane Figures

Fill in the ◯ for the correct answer.

1   Which is a triangle?

    A   **B**    **C**

2   How many sides does a rectangle have?

    A   1   **B**   3   **C**   4

3   Which does not have a line of symmetry?

    A    **B**   **C**

4   Which figure is congruent to ⬚ ?

    A 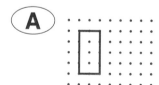   **B** 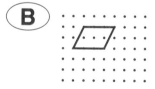   **C**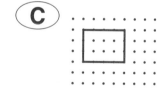

5   Which shows a slide?

    A    **B** 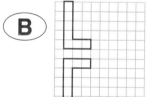   **C**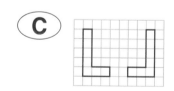

6   Which shows a turn?

    A   **B**   **C**

PRACTICE ANSWERS
Page 143

1. triangle
2. rectangle
3. circle
4. rectangle
5. triangle
6. circle
7. yes
8. no
9. yes
10. 3
11. 6
12. 4

Page 145

1. flip
2. slide
3. turn
4. flip
5. turn
6. slide

Page 146

1. B
2. C
3. B
4. A
5. A
6. C

Page 144

1. Answers will vary.
   Sample answers:

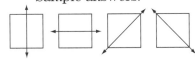

2. Answers will vary.
   Sample answers:

3.

4.

5.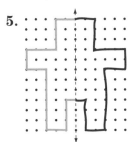

6. yes
7. no
8. no

Name _____ Date _____

204 Solid Figures

Write the name of each figure.

Word Bank		
sphere	cube	cone
rectangular prism	cylinder	pyramid

1

_____

2

_____

3

_____

4

_____

5

_____

6

_____

Write About Math

7 Make a list of things that have the shape of a rectangular prism.

_____

_____

Name _____ Date _____

205 **Circle the solid figure you you can use to draw each plane figure.**

I can use this cube to draw a square.

1

2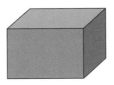

3

4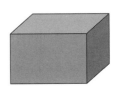

Math to Learn

Name _____ Date _____

Solid Figures

Fill in the ◯ **for the correct answer.**

1 Which is a cube?

Ⓐ

Ⓑ

Ⓒ

2 Which is a cylinder?

Ⓐ

Ⓑ

Ⓒ

3 Which is a sphere?

Ⓐ

Ⓑ

Ⓒ

4 Which face is on a cone?

Ⓐ

Ⓑ

Ⓒ

5 Which face is on a rectangular prism?

Ⓐ

Ⓑ

Ⓒ

6 Which face is on a square pyramid?

Ⓐ

Ⓑ

Ⓒ

PRACTICE ANSWERS
Page 148

1. cube
2. pyramid
3. sphere
4. cone
5. rectangular prism
6. cylinder
7. Answers will vary. Sample answers: cereal box, raisin box, gift box, toy box/chest, block of cheese, blocks, toaster, shoe box, suitcase

Page 149

1.
triangle

2.
circle

3.
circle

4.
rectangle

TEST PREP ANSWERS
Page 150

1. A
2. C
3. C
4. B
5. B
6. A

Tangrams and Triangles

OBJECTIVES
- Use slides, flips, and turns
- Arrange shapes to form triangles
- Use the Guess, Check, and Revise problem-solving strategy

MATERIALS
- Commercial tangrams, or copies made from the blackline master on page 224

TIME
- 30–40 minutes

TEACHER NOTES
- Ask children to use the two large triangles to form:

1. a square

2. another figure with 4 sides

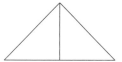

3. a larger triangle

- Choose a way for children to record the triangles they make when doing the activity on page 153. They can either trace the pieces or you can make multiple copies of page 224, and children can cut and paste the pieces.

EXTENSION
- Have students make a shape with two or more tangram pieces, trace along the outline of the shape, and then have a classmate use the tangram pieces to try to figure out how the shape was made.

ANSWERS
Two ways to make triangles are shown on page 153. Here are 11 more ways. (Note: Children's triangles may differ from these, since the same pieces can sometimes be arranged in different configurations.)

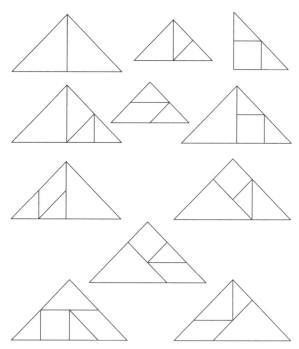

You may wish to use this **scoring rubric** to assess students' work.

3 points	• Student records at least 3 different ways to make a triangle.
2 points	• Student records at least 2 different ways to make a triangle.
1 point	• Student records fewer than 2 different ways to make a triangle.

Name _____ Date _____

Names of Plane Figures
pages 196–197

Congruent Figures
pages 200–201

Slides, Flips, and Turns
pages 202–203

Tangrams and Triangles

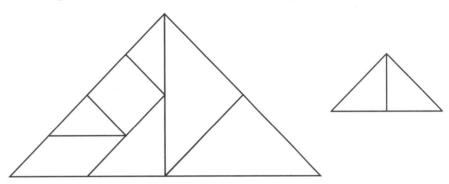

Here are two ways to make a triangle using at least 2 tangram pieces. See how many other ways you can find to make triangles.

Show the different ways here and on the back of this paper.

Use other sheets of paper if you need to.

Name _____ Date _____

Length

208 | **Circle the answer.**

1 Which is longer?

2 Which is shorter?

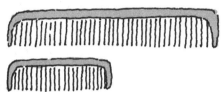

3 Which is longest?

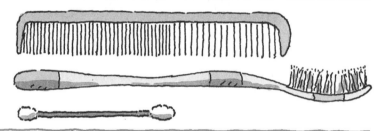

4 Which is tallest?

5 Which is shortest?

209

6 How many hair pins long is the toothpaste tube?

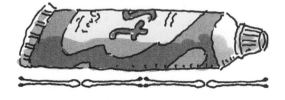

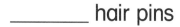

_____ hair pins

Name _____ Date _____

210–211 **Complete. Use a customary unit of length.**

Customary Units of Length

inch   foot   yard

---

1 This paper is about 1 _____ long.

2 A paper clip is about 1 _____ long.

3 A baseball bat is about 1 _____ long.

4 Mark the place on the ruler where you would place one end of something you might measure.

0 inches   1   2

5 Estimate and then measure the length of 3 objects. Write the units you used—inches, feet, or yards.

Object	Estimate	Length
_____	_____	_____
_____	_____	_____
_____	_____	_____

Name _____ Date _____

212–213 **Complete. Use a metric unit of length.**

Metric Units of Length	
centimeter	meter

1 The distance from the floor to the doorknob

is about 1 _____.

2 The width of a fingernail is about 1 _____.

3 How many centimeters are in 1 meter? _____ centimeters

4 Estimate. Then measure the lengths in centimeters.

Object	Estimate	Length
Width of your hand	_____	_____
Your height	_____	_____
Your pace	_____	_____

Name _____ Date _____

Length

1   Circle the one that is longer.

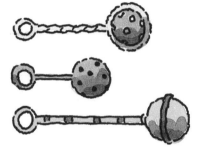

2   Circle the one that is longest.

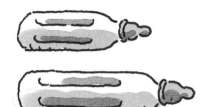

3   Circle the one that is tallest.

4   How many bottles long is the baby?

_____ bottles long

Name _____ Date _____

Length

1 Which is lined up correctly to measure? Circle it.

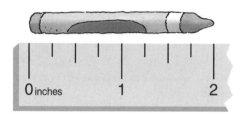
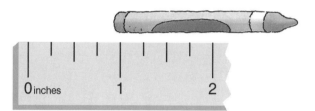

Use a ruler to measure each item. Write the length.

2

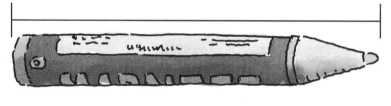

_____ inches

3

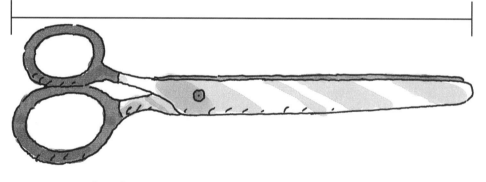

_____ inches

4

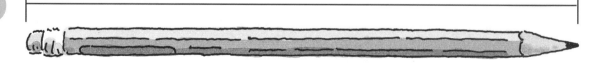

_____ inches

Name _____ Date _____

Length

Use a centimeter ruler to measure each item.
Circle the letter next to the best length.

 1

A. 4 centimeters

B. 9 centimeters

C. 20 centimeters

 2

A. 15 centimeters

B. 6 centimeters

C. 25 centimeters

3

A. 8 centimeters

B. 12 centimeters

C. 3 centimeters

4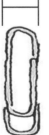

A. 5 centimeters

B. 1 centimeter

C. 10 centimeters

Math to Learn

PRACTICE ANSWERS
Page 154

1.

2.

3.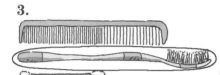

4.

5.

6. 4

Page 155

1. foot
2. inch
3. yard
4.

5. Answers will vary. Check for the reasonableness of the lengths.

Page 156

1. meter
2. centimeter
3. 100
4. Estimates may vary greatly. Accept all estimates, other than estimates that are exactly the same as the actual lengths, which would indicate that students did not really estimate before measuring. Actual lengths may be about

Width of your hand	5-10 cm
Your height	80-120 cm
Your pace	30-50 cm

TEST PREP ANSWERS
Page 157

1.

2.

3.

4. 4

TEST PREP ANSWERS
Page 158

1.

2. 4 inches
3. 5 inches
4. 6 inches

Page 159

1. B
2. A
3. C
4. B

Name _____ Date _____

Perimeter and Area

Perimeter is the distance around a figure.

214–215 **Find the perimeter of each figure.**

 1

The perimeter is _____ toothpicks.

 **2**

3 feet | 5 feet

4 feet

The perimeter is _____ feet.

 3

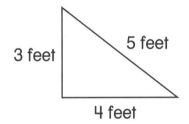

The perimeter is _____ toothpicks.

4

1 inch

3 inches

The perimeter is _____ inches.

Name _____ Date _____

Area is the number of square units you need to cover a figure.

216 **Find the area of each figure.**

1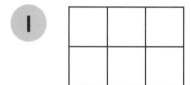

The area is _____ square units.

2

The area is _____ square units.

3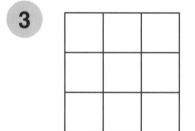

The area is _____ square units.

4

The area is _____ square units.

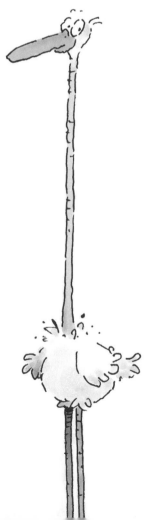

Name _____ Date _____

Perimeter and Area

Fill in the next to the correct answer.

Find the perimeter of each figure.

1

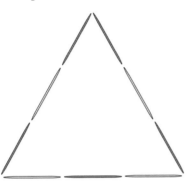

- **A** 3 toothpicks
- **B** 9 toothpicks
- **C** 6 toothpicks

2

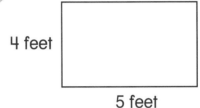

4 feet

5 feet

- **A** 8 feet
- **B** 9 feet
- **C** 18 feet

Find the area of each figure.

3

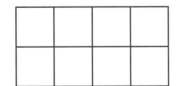

- **A** 8 square units
- **B** 6 square units
- **C** 12 square units

4

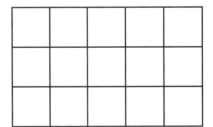

- **A** 8 square units
- **B** 15 square units
- **C** 16 square units

PRACTICE ANSWERS
Page 161
1. 6
2. 12
3. 6
4. 8

Page 162
1. 6
2. 12
3. 9
4. 10

TEST PREP ANSWERS
Page 163
1. B
2. C
3. A
4. B

Name _____ Date _____

Weight and Mass

218–219 Write the customary unit of weight that seems more reasonable.

Customary Units of Weight	
ounce	pound

1

I _____

2

54 _____s

3

I _____

4

5 _____s

5 Circle the object that weighs more.

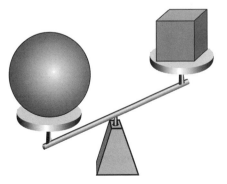

Name _____ Date _____

220–221 **Write the metric unit of mass that seems more reasonable.**

Metric Units of Mass	
gram	kilogram

1

I _____

2

35 _____s

3

I5 _____s

4

I _____

Name _____ Date _____

Weight and Mass

Circle the more reasonable weight or mass.

1

A. 8 ounces

B. 8 pounds

2

A. 6 ounces

B. 6 pounds

3

A. 25 kilograms

B. 25 grams

4

A. 5 kilograms

B. 5 grams

5 Which is heavier?

A. rabbit

B. carrot

Math to Learn

PRACTICE ANSWERS
Page 165

1. ounce
2. pounds
3. pound
4. ounces
5.

Page 166

1. gram
2. kilograms
3. kilograms
4. kilogram

TEST PREP ANSWERS
Page 167

1. B
2. A
3. A
4. B
5. A

Name _____ Date _____

222–223 # Capacity

1 Circle the containers that hold about 1 cup.

2 Circle the containers that hold about 1 pint.

3 Circle the containers that hold about 1 quart.

Name _____ Date _____

224–225

1 Circle the container that holds about 5 milliliters.

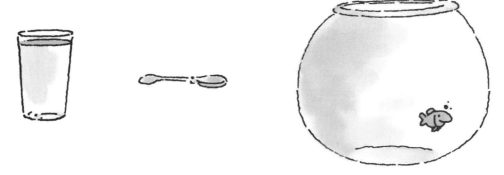

2 Circle the container that holds about 1 liter.

**Does the container hold more or less than 1 liter?
Write *more* or *less*.**

3 swimming pool _____

4 drinking glass _____

5 tablespoon _____

6 bathtub _____

Name _____ Date _____

Capacity

How much does the container hold?
Circle the best answer.

1

A. about 1 cup

B. about 1 quart

2

A. about 1 cup

B. about 1 quart

3

A. more than 1 pint

B. less than 1 pint

4

A. about 5 liters

B. about 5 milliliters

5

A. about 1 milliliter

B. about 1 liter

6

A. more than 1 liter

B. less than 1 liter

PRACTICE ANSWERS
Page 169

1.

2.

3.

Page 170

1.

2.

3. more
4. less
5. less
6. more

TEST PREP ANSWERS
Page 171

1. B
2. A
3. B
4. B
5. B
6. A

Name _____ Date _____

Temperature

226–227 **Draw a line from the temperature to the correct picture.**

When the temperature goes up, it is getting warmer.

1 20°F •

•

2 80°F •

•

Write About Math

3 Write and draw about your favorite weather. Color the thermometer to match your story.

_____

_____

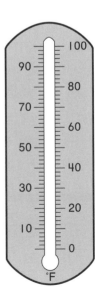

Name _____ Date _____

228–229 **Draw a line from the temperature to the correct picture.**

When the temperature goes down, it is getting cooler.

1 20°C •

2 0°C •

Color the thermometer to match the temperature.

3

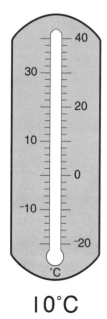

10°C

4

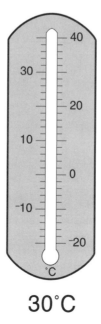

30°C

5

24°C

Name _____ Date _____

Temperature

Circle the best answer.

1 When the temperature "goes up," the weather is getting

   A. warmer   **B.** cooler

---

2 Which thermometer shows the cooler temperature?

   A.    **B.**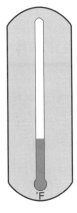

---

3 What is the temperature?

   A. 70°F

   B. 80°F

4 What is the temperature?

   A. 20°C

   B. 10°C

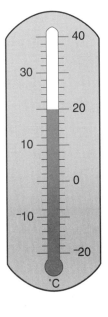

Math to Learn

PRACTICE ANSWERS
Page 173

1.

2.

3. Stories and temperatures will vary. Check for reasonableness.

Page 174

1.

2.

3.

4.

5.

TEST PREP ANSWERS
Page 175

1. A
2. B
3. B
4. A

Name _____ Date _____

Measurement Tools and Units

230–231 **You have a glass of water. Draw a line from what you measure to the measuring tool you would use.**

1 Height of the water •

•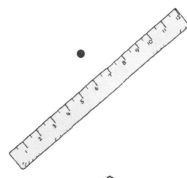

2 Weight of the water and glass •

•

3 How much water is in the glass •

•

4 Temperature of the water •

•

5 Would you measure the height of the water in inches or yards?

Name _____ Date _____

Measurement Tools and Units

Circle the best answer.

1 Which tool would you use to find out how tall you are?

A.   **B.**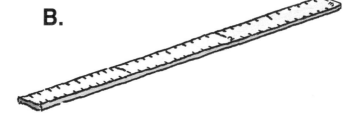

2 Which tool would you use to find out how much you weigh?

A.    **B.**

3 Which tool would you use to find out how much juice you have?

A.    **B.**

4 Which unit would you use to measure your height?

A. inches   **B.** pounds

PRACTICE ANSWERS
Page 177

1. ruler
2. scale
3. measuring cup
4. thermometer
5. inches

TEST PREP ANSWERS
Page 178

1. B
2. A
3. B
4. A

Treasure Map

OBJECTIVE
- Measure using nonstandard units of length
- Measure using customary or metric units of length
- Follow directions on a map
- Write directions using a map

MATERIALS
- inch or centimeter rulers, paper clips
- colored pencils

TIME
- 30–40 minutes

TEACHER NOTES
- Read the following directions to the students. Help them mark the path on page 181 as you read.

  Begin at Start.

  Go east 3 centimeters. (Have students use a centimeter ruler to check that each side of a square measures 1 centimeter.)

  Go south 5 centimeters.

  Go west 1 centimeter.

  Go south 3 centimeters.

  Go east 3 centimeters.

  Go south 2 centimeters.

  Go east 1 centimeters.

  Go south 3 centimeters.

- Have students choose a treasure first, and then write directions to the treasure. Tell them to keep their chosen treasure a secret, writing it on the back of the direction sheet. When they complete writing and checking their directions, they can exchange them with classmates who can follow the directions to find the treasure.

- Students should use a different color pencil each time they begin to make or follow a new set of directions.

- If a student is unable to write clearly, he/she can give verbal directions to a chosen treasure.

EXTENSION
- Have students make a new grid using inches or a non-standard unit of measurement such as a paper clip. They can then use the new grid to make a different set of directions to a treasure.

ANSWERS
1. Treasure B

2. Check students' directions.

You may wish to use this **scoring rubric** to assess students' work.

3 points	• Student's written or verbal directions lead to a treasure.
2 points	• Student's written or verbal directions contain one or two errors and do not lead to a treasure.
1 point	• Student's written or verbal directions contain three or more errors and do not lead to a treasure.

Name _____ Date _____

Treasure Map

Follow the directions from your teacher to find Treasure A, B, or C. The compass can help you figure out which way to turn.

START

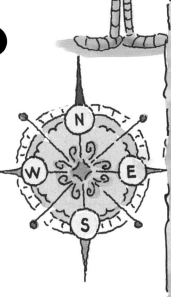

Length
pages 208-212

Measurement Tools
and Units
pages 230-231

Use a separate sheet of paper to write your own set of directions.

1 Which treasure did you find? _____

2 Make your own set of directions to one of the three treasures.

Math to Learn

Name _____ Date _____

Graphing and Statistics

234 **Use the tally chart to answer the questions.**

What is your favorite pizza topping?

Topping	Tally
Pepperoni	//// //// //
Mushroom	//// //

1 How many children prefer mushroom? _____

2 How many children prefer pepperoni? _____

3 How many more children prefer pepperoni than mushroom? _____

235 **Use the table to answer the questions.**

What did you drink for lunch today?

	Juice	Milk
Boys	3	5
Girls	2	4
Total	5	9

4 How many boys had milk? _____

5 How many more girls drank milk than juice? _____

6 How many children had juice? _____

Name _____ Date _____

236 **Use the picture graph to answer the questions.**

What color apple do you prefer?

| Green | 🍏 | 🍏 | | | | |
| Red | 🍎 | 🍎 | 🍎 | 🍎 | 🍎 | 🍎 |

1 Which color apple did more children choose? _____

2 How many more children chose red than green? _____

238–239

3 Make a bar graph using the information above. Label your graph.

Title _____

Color

Green

Red

0 ____ ____ ____ ____ ____ ____

Number of _____

Name _____ Date _____

240–241 **Use the pictograph to answer the questions.**

What is your favorite potato topping?

Butter	😊	😊	😊	😊	😊	
Cheese	😊	😊	😊			
Sour Cream	😊	😊	🙂			

Key 😊 = 2 children

1 What does one 😊 stand for? _____

2 How many children chose butter? _____

3 What does 🙂 stand for? _____

4 How many children chose sour cream? _____

5 How many more children chose cheese than chose sour cream? _____

Name _____ Date _____

242–243　**Use the Venn diagram to answer the questions.**

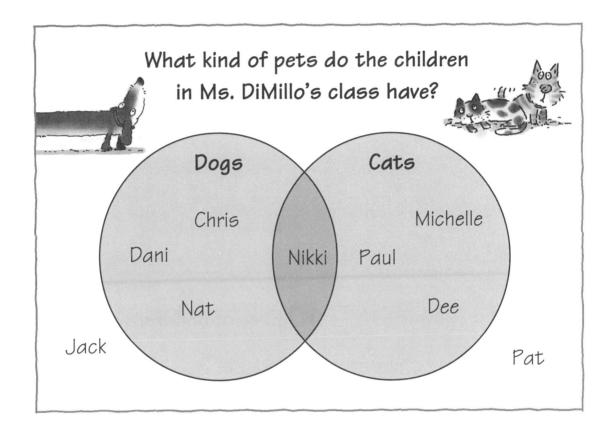

What kind of pets do the children
in Ms. DiMillo's class have?

Dogs　　　　　Cats

Chris　　　　　　　Michelle

Dani　　　　Nikki　Paul

Nat　　　　　　　　Dee

Jack　　　　　　　　　　　　Pat

1　Which children do not have a dog or a cat?

_____ _____

2　How many children have only a dog? _____

3　How many children have a cat? _____

4　Which child has both a dog and a cat? _____

Name _____ Date _____

Graphing and Statistics

Use the bar graph to answer the questions.

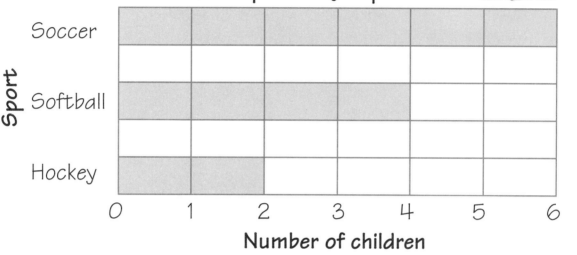

Which sport do you prefer?

Number of children

1. How many children chose soccer? _____

2. How many more children chose softball than hockey? _____

Use the tally chart to answer the questions.

3. How many children came to soccer practice on Tuesday?

_____

How many children came to soccer practice?

| Tuesday | ⅼⅼⅼⅼⅼ ⅼⅼⅼⅼⅼ ⅼ |
| Thursday | ⅼⅼⅼⅼⅼ ⅼⅼⅼⅼ |

4. How many more children came to soccer practice on Tuesday than on Thursday? _____

Name _____ Date _____

Graphing and Statistics

Use the pictograph to answer the questions.

Books Sold at Book Sale

Room 1	📘	📘	📘	📘		
Room 2	📘	📘	📘	📘	📘	📘
Room 3	📘	📘	📘	📘		

1 What does one 📘 stand for?   Key 📘 = 2 books

_____

2 How many books did Room 1 sell? _____

3 How many more books did Room 2 sell than Room 1? _____

4 How many books did Room 3 sell? _____

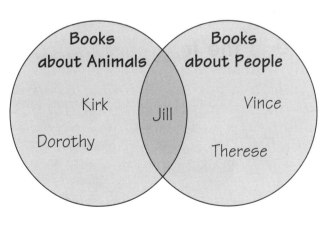

Books about Animals   Books about People

Kirk   Jill   Vince

Dorothy   Therese

Use the Venn diagram to answer the questions.

5 How many people bought books only about animals? _____

6 How many people bought books about animals and books about people? _____

Math to Learn

PRACTICE ANSWERS
Page 182
  1. 7
  2. 12
  3. 5
  4. 5
  5. 2
  6. 5

Page 183
  1. red
  2. 4

3.

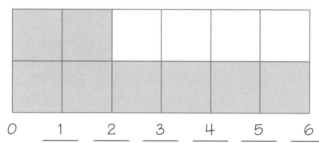

Title ___What color apple do you prefer?___

Color — Green — Red

0 1 2 3 4 5 6

Number of _____ children

Page 184
  1. 2 children
  2. 10
  3. 1 child
  4. 5
  5. 1

Page 185
  1. Jack, Pat
  2. 3
  3. 4
  4. Nikki

TEST PREP ANSWERS
Page 186
  1. 6
  2. 2
  3. 11
  4. 2

Page 187
  1. 2 books
  2. 8
  3. 4
  4. 7
  5. 2
  6. 1

Name _____ Date _____

Probability

244–249 **Color the spinners and answer the questions.**

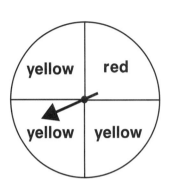

1 What color is the arrow more likely to land on?

_____

2 What color is the arrow less likely to land on?

_____

3 What color is impossible for the arrow to land on?

_____

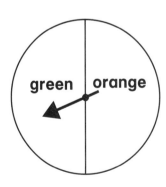

4 Is it possible for the arrow to land on orange?

_____

5 How likely is it that the arrow will land on green? Circle the best answer.

impossible   certain   equally likely as orange

Math to Learn

Name _____ Date _____

Probability

Color the spinners. Circle the best answer.

1 How likely is it that the arrow will land on purple?

A. certain

B. unlikely

2 How likely is it that the arrow will land on yellow?

A. likely

B. unlikely

3 How likely is it that the arrow will land on red?

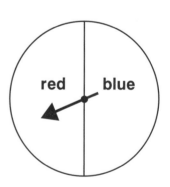

A. certain

B. equally likely as blue

4 How likely is it that the arrow will land on brown?

A. certain

B. impossible

Math to Learn

PRACTICE ANSWERS
Page 187

1. yellow

2. red

3. Answers will vary; accept any color except red or yellow.

4. yes

5. equally likely as orange

TEST PREP ANSWERS
Page 188

1. B

2. A

3. B

4. B

Survey Your Classmates

OBJECTIVES
• Collect data
• Make a tally chart
• Make a graph

MATERIALS
• colored pencils or markers for graphs

TIME
• 30–40 minutes

TEACHER NOTES
• Introduce the idea of a survey by asking a question and keeping track of students' responses on a tally chart. Develop some possible yes/no questions students can ask when they conduct their own surveys.

Do you like strawberries? (chocolate? mustard? sauerkraut? artichokes? rainy days? dressing up in your best clothes?)

Did you drink any milk yet today?

Do you write with your left hand?

Fold your hands. Is your right thumb on top?

Did you walk to school today? (ride the bus? come in a car?

Do you have a little sister? (little brother? big brother? big sister? dog? cat?)

EXTENSIONS
• Have students write sentences to tell some things their bar graphs show.

• Have students show the same data using a pictograph.

You may wish to use this **scoring rubric** to assess students' work.

3 points	• Student collects data and records results using tally marks. • Student makes a graph that displays survey results correctly.
2 points	• Student collects data and records results using tally marks. • Student makes some errors in displaying the survey results on the graph.
1 point	• Student does not formulate a question and/or does not collect any data.

Name _____ Date _____

Survey Your Classmates

1 Think of a yes/no question to ask some of your classmates. Make a tally chart to keep track of their answers.

HANDBOOK HELP

Tally Charts
page 234

Bar graphs
pages 238–239

Question: _____

Answer	Tally Marks	Number
Yes		
No		

2 Make a bar graph to show what you learned about your classmates. Label the parts of your graph.

Title _____

Answer

Yes

No

0   ____ ____ ____ ____ ____ ____

Number of _____

Math to Learn

Name _____ Date _____

254–255 # Patterns and Functions

        ?
_____

1   Which comes next? Circle it.

2   Which will be the 12th animal? Circle it.

---

3   Which animal will start Row 10? Circle it.

Row 1	🐻	🐰	🐻
Row 2	🐰	🐻	🐰
Row 3	🐻	🐰	🐻
Row 4	🐰	🐻	🐰

Name _____ Date _____

256–257 **Look at this pattern.**

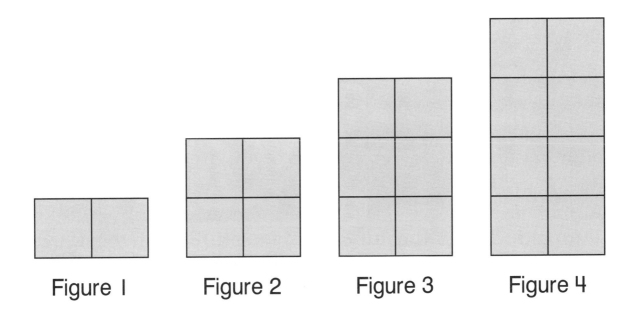

Figure 1   Figure 2   Figure 3   Figure 4

1 How many squares will be in Figure 5? _____

2 Complete the table.

Figure number	1	2	3	4	5	6	7
Number of squares	2	4					

3 How many squares will be in Figure 8?

_____

Name _____ Date _____

256–257 **Complete the function tables.**

1

Rule: + 1	
In	Out
3	4
7	
4	
0	

2

Rule: + 2	
In	Out
4	6
5	
0	
9	

3

Rule: + 2	
In	Out
7	
	5
1	
	8

4

Rule: − 1	
In	Out
4	3
8	
2	
6	

5

Rule: − 2	
In	Out
9	7
3	
10	
5	

6

Rule: − 2	
In	Out
8	
	2
7	
	7

Name _____ Date _____

Patterns and Functions

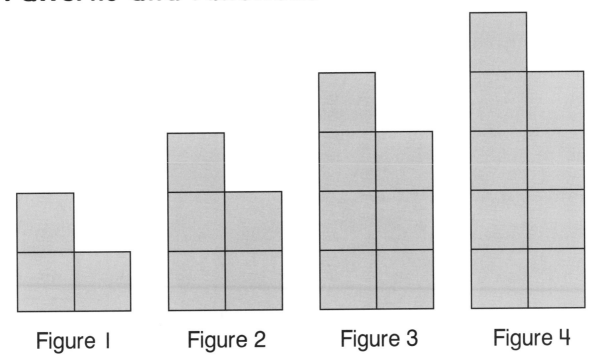

Figure 1   Figure 2   Figure 3   Figure 4

1 How many squares will be in Figure 5? _____

2 Complete the table.

Figure number	1	2	3	4	5	6	7
Number of squares	3	5					

3 How many squares will be in Figure 8?

_____

Math to Learn

Name _____ Date _____

Patterns and Functions

1 Which animal will start Row 4? Circle it.

Row 1	🐘	🦆	🦆	🐘
Row 2	🦆	🦆	🐘	🦆
Row 3	🦆	🐘	🦆	🦆

2

Rule: + 2	
In	Out
2	4
5	
1	
6	

3

Rule: − 2	
In	Out
3	1
7	
5	
8	

4

Rule: + 1	
In	Out
3	
	7
2	
	4

**PRACTICE ANSWERS
Page 194**

1.

2.

3.

Page 195

1. 10

2.

Figure number	1	2	3	4	5	6	7
Number of squares	2	4	6	8	10	12	14

3. 16

Page 196

1.

Rule: + 1	
In	Out
3	4
7	8
4	5
0	1

2.

Rule: + 2	
In	Out
4	6
5	7
0	2
9	11

3.

Rule: + 2	
In	Out
7	9
3	5
1	3
6	8

4.

Rule: − 1	
In	Out
4	3
8	7
2	1
6	5

5.

Rule: − 2	
In	Out
9	7
3	1
10	8
5	3

6.

Rule: − 2	
In	Out
8	6
4	2
7	5
9	7

**TEST PREP ANSWERS
Page 197**

1. 11

2.

Figure number	1	2	3	4	5	6	7
Number of squares	3	5	7	9	11	13	15

3. 17

**TEST PREP ANSWERS
Page 198**

1.

2.

Rule: + 2	
In	Out
2	4
5	7
1	3
6	8

3.

Rule: − 2	
In	Out
3	1
7	5
5	3
8	6

4.

Rule: − 2	
In	Out
3	4
6	7
2	3
3	4

Name _____ Date _____

258–260 **Equations**

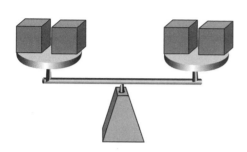 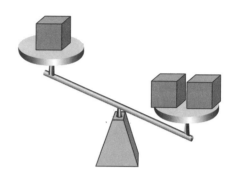

① Circle the scale that is balanced.

② Draw a line under the scale that is not balanced.
Circle the side that is heavier.

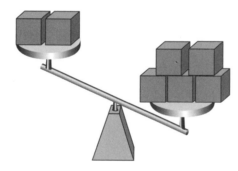

③ Circle the side that is heavier.

④ How many cubes will you need to put
on the lighter side to balance the scale?

_____

Name _____ Date _____

258–260

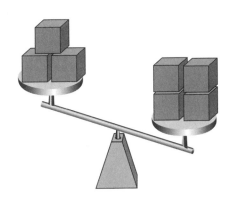

1 Circle the side that is heavier.

2 How many cubes will you need to put
   on the lighter side to balance the scale? _____

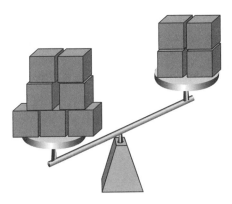

3 Circle the side that is heavier.

4 How many cubes will you need to put
   on the lighter side to balance the scale? _____

5 $4 + \underline{\hspace{1cm}} = 7$

Math to Learn

Name _____ Date _____

261

1 How much does the truck weigh? _____

2 How much do the truck and doll weigh in all?

_____

3 How much does the doll weigh? _____

Write the missing number.

4 5 + _____ = 9

5 2 + _____ = 3

6 7 + _____ = 8

7 _____ + 4 = 7

8 _____ + 3 = 5

9 6 = _____ + 4

10 7 = 5 + _____

11 8 = 7 + _____

12 2 + 1 = 1 + _____

13 2 + 3 = 4 + _____

Name _____ Date _____

Equations

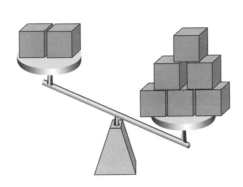

1 Circle the side that is heavier.

2 How many cubes will you need to put
on the lighter side to balance the scale? _____

3 How much does the boat weigh? _____

4 How much do the boat and dolphin weigh in all?

_____

5 How much does the dolphin weigh? _____

Write the missing number.

6 $3 + \underline{\hspace{1cm}} = 8$ 7 $9 + \underline{\hspace{1cm}} = 10$

Math to Learn

PRACTICE ANSWERS
Page 200

1–2.

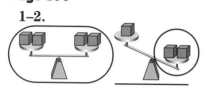

3.

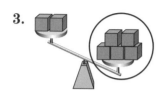

4. 3

Page 201

1.

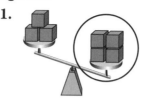

2. 1

3.

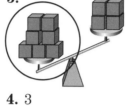

4. 3

5. 3

Page 202

1. 5 pounds
2. 9 pounds
3. 4 pounds
4. 4
5. 1
6. 1
7. 3
8. 2
9. 2
10. 2
11. 1
12. 2
13. 1

TEST PREP ANSWERS
Page 203

1.

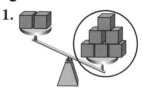

2. 4
3. 3 pounds
4. 8 pounds
5. 5 pounds
6. 5   7. 1

Name _____ Date _____

Properties

262

1   2 + 3 = _____   **2**   3 + 2 = _____

3   Does the sum change when you change the order of addends? _____

Add the two numbers that are underlined first.

4 $\underline{3} + \underline{1} + 7 =$ _____   **5** $3 + \underline{1} + \underline{7} =$ _____

6   Did the sum change? _____

Write each sum.

7   7 + 0 = _____   **8**   0 + 8 = _____

9   87 + 0 = _____   **10**   0 + 42 = _____

11   What happens when you add zero to a number?

_____

Name _____ Date _____

263

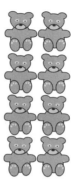

1 $2 \times 4 =$ _____ **2** $4 \times 2 =$ _____

3 Does the product change when you change the order of factors? _____

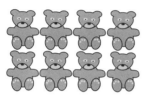

3 groups with 1 bear

1 group with 3 bears

4 $3 \times 1 =$ _____ **5** $1 \times 3 =$ _____

6 What happens when you multiply a number by 1?

_____

2 plates with 0 cookies   0 plates with 2 cookies

7 $2 \times 0 =$ _____ **8** $0 \times 2 =$ _____

9 What happens when you multiply a number by 0?

_____

Name _____ Date _____

Properties

Fill in the ◯ for the correct answer.

1 $2 + 3$
has the same answer as

   Ⓐ $2 + 0$

   Ⓑ $2 + 1$

   Ⓒ $3 + 2$

2 $3 + 4 + 2$
has the same answer as

   Ⓐ $2 + 4 + 3$

   Ⓑ $2 + 1 + 4$

   Ⓒ $4 + 1 + 2$

3 $2 + 0 = $ _____

   Ⓐ 0

   Ⓑ 2

   Ⓒ 1

4 2×3
has the same answer as

   Ⓐ $2 + 3$

   Ⓑ 3×2

   Ⓒ $3 - 2$

5 $5 \times 1 = $ _____

   Ⓐ 5

   Ⓑ 2

   Ⓒ 0

6 $4 \times 0 = $ _____

   Ⓐ 4

   Ⓑ 0

   Ⓒ 40

PRACTICE ANSWERS
Page 205

1. 5
2. 5
3. no
4. 11
5. 11
6. no
7. 7
8. 8
9. 87
10. 42
11. When you add zero to a number, the sum is that same number.

Page 206

1. 8
2. 8
3. no
4. 3
5. 3
6. When you multiply a number by 1, the number stays the same.
7. 0
8. 0
9. When you multiply a number by 0, the product is 0.

TEST PREP ANSWERS
Page 207

1. C
2. A
3. B
4. B
5. A
6. B

Name _____ Date _____

264–265 **Coordinate Graphs**

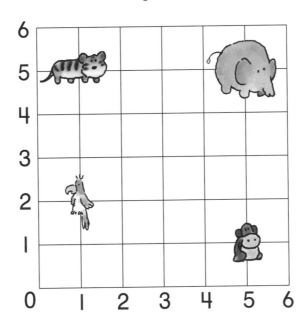

1. What ordered pair tells where is? _____

2. What ordered pair tells where is? _____

3. What ordered pair tells where  is? _____

Write About Math

4. Are (1, 5) and (5, 1) the same? Explain.

_____

_____

Name _____ Date _____

Coordinate Graphs

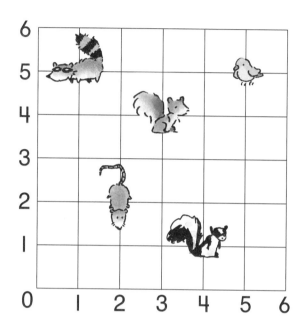

1 What ordered pair tells where is? _____

2 What ordered pair tells where is? _____

3 What ordered pair tells where is? _____

4 What ordered pair tells where is? _____

5 What ordered pair tells where is? _____

PRACTICE ANSWERS
Page 209

1. (1, 2)
2. (5, 1)
3. (1, 5)
4. No. Reasons will vary. Sample: (5, 1) tells where the monkey is and (1, 5) tells where the tiger is.

TEST PREP ANSWERS
Page 210

1. (1, 5)
2. (4, 1)
3. (2, 2)
4. (3, 4)
5. (5, 5)

Shapes and Ordered Pairs

OBJECTIVES
- Use ordered pairs to find points on a graph
- Use ordered pairs to name points on a graph
- Recognize and name closed, plane figures

MATERIALS
- none

TIME
- 30–40 minutes

TEACHER NOTES
- Write the ordered pair (2, 1) on the board. Ask students to use the grid on page 213 to place a dot on the location of (2, 1). Check to be sure students have placed the point correctly. Then have students complete the rest of the activity independently.

EXTENSION
Encourage students to create other ordered-pair puzzles to share with their classmates. They can make other geometric figures or their own designs. They may wish to make letters of the alphabet.

ANSWERS
1. hexagon

2. Answers will vary. Check students' work.

You may wish to use this **scoring rubric** to assess students' work.

3 points	• Student finds and connects points and identifies the hexagon. • Student writes ordered pairs that can be connected to form a rectangle.
2 points	• Student is not able to identify the shape as a hexagon and/or • Student makes 1 to 4 errors in plotting points and identifying ordered pairs.
1 point	• Student makes more than 4 errors in plotting points and identifying ordered pairs.

Name _____ Date _____

Shapes and Ordered Pairs

1 Make a dot at each ordered pair.

(2, 1) (1, 3) (2, 4) (4, 4) (5, 3) (4, 1)

Connect the dots to make a closed figure.

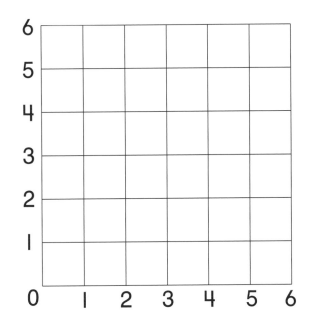

What shape did you make?

_____

2 Write ordered pairs for the corners
of a rectangle.

_____   _____

_____   _____

Name _____ Date _____

Problem-Solving Strategies

272–273 **Use counters to act out this problem.**

1 3 girls are in the play.

2 more boys than girls are in the play.

How many children are in the play? _____

274–275 **Draw a picture to solve this problem.**

2 7 girls are at a party.

2 of the girls wear blue.

1 girl wears yellow.

The rest of the girls wear red.

How many girls wear red? _____

276–277 **Find a pattern.**

3 Draw the next two items in this pattern.

Name _____ Date _____

278–279   **Guess, check, and revise to solve this problem.**

1   There a re 5 animals in the barn.
They have 14 legs in all.
Some are cows and some are chickens.
How many are cows and how many are chickens?

_____ cows and _____ chickens

280–281   **Make a list to solve this problem.**

2   How many different ways can you dress
the the bear? (Use a shirt and pants for each way.)

282–284   **Complete the table to solve this problem.**

3   How many sandwiches can you
make with 12 slices of bread? _____

Sandwiches	1	2	3				
Slices of bread	2						

Math to Learn

Name _____ Date _____

Problem-Solving Strategies

Draw a picture to solve this problem.

1 There are 3 dogs at the park.
2 more dogs come to the park.
How many dogs are there now? _____

Look for a pattern.

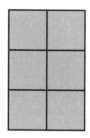

2 How many squares will be in the next stack? _____

3 Guess and check to find the numbers
for , ▲, and ●.

$\blacksquare + \blacktriangle = 7$

$\blacksquare + \bullet = 8$

$\blacktriangle + \bullet = 11$

$\blacksquare = $ _____ $\blacktriangle = $ _____ $\bullet = $ _____

PRACTICE ANSWERS
Page 214

1. 8

2. 4

3. △□□△□□△□□△□

Pages 215

1. 2 cows and 3 chickens

2. 6

yellow jacket-blue pants

yellow jacket-green pants

yellow jacket- red pants

red jacket-blue pants

red jacket- green pants

red jacket- red pants

3. 6

Sandwiches	1	2	3	4	5	6	7
Slices of bread	2	4	6	8	10	12	14

TEST PREP ANSWERS
Page 216

1. 5

2. 8

3. ■ = 2

△ = 5

● = 6

Name _____ Date _____

Problem-Solving Skills

286–289 **Circle add or subtract to show how you would solve each problem.**

1 There are 5 birds in the tree.
2 fly away.
How many birds are in the tree now?

| add |
| subtract |

2 There are 5 birds in the nest.
2 big birds fly to the nest.
How many are there now?

| add |
| subtract |

3 Mama bird puts 5 worms in the nest.
Baby birds eat 2 of the worms.
How many worms are there now?

| add |
| subtract |

Circle subtract or multiply to show how you would solve the problem.

4 There are 5 nests.
2 birds are in each nest.
How many birds are there in all?

| subtract |
| multiply |

Name _____ Date _____

290–296 **Solve.**

1 5 puppies are in the basket.
Mark put 1 more puppy in the basket.
His sister takes 2 of the puppies out.
How many puppies are in the basket now? _____

2 You buy a  and a
for your puppies.
You give the clerk a quarter.
How much change do you get? _____

3 Use the clues to find the number.

1   2   3   4   5   6   7   8   9   10

• It is less than 8.

• It is an even number.

• It is more than 4.

The number is _____.

4 Nikki's soccer team has 12 players.
They buy 2 shirts for each player.
How many shirts does the team buy?
Circle the answer that makes sense.

14   10   24

Name _____ Date _____

Problem-Solving Skills

Fill in the ⬭ to show how you would solve each problem.

1 There are 5 math books and 3 reading books. How many more math books than reading books are there?

   A $5 + 3 = 8$ **B** $5 - 3 = 2$ **C** $5 \times 3 = 15$

2 There are 5 math books and 3 reading books. How many books there?

   A $5 + 3 = 8$ **B** $5 - 3 = 2$ **C** $5 \times 3 = 15$

3 There are 5 math books in Kelly's room. Kelly takes 3 of the books to another room. How many books are in Kelly's room now?

   A $5 + 3 = 8$ **B** $5 - 3 = 2$ **C** $5 \times 3 = 15$

4 There are 5 math books on each shelf. There are 3 shelves. How many math books are there?

   A $5 + 3 = 8$ **B** $5 - 3 = 2$ **C** $5 \times 3 = 15$

PRACTICE ANSWERS
Page 218

1. subtract
2. add
3. subtract
4. multiply

Page 219

1. 4
2. 10¢
3. 6

Encourage children to cross out information as they get clues.

- It is less than 8.

1 2 3 4 5 6 7 X̶ X̶ X̶

- It is an even number.

X̶ 2 X̶ 4 X̶ 6 X̶ X̶ X̶

- It is more than 4.

X̶ X̶ X̶ X̶ X̶ 6 X̶ X̶ X̶

4. 24

TEST PREP ANSWERS
Page 220

1. B
2. A
3. B
4. C

Story Problems for Graphs

OBJECTIVES
- Use data from graphs to write story problems
- Write and solve story problems

MATERIALS
- none

TIME
- 30–40 minutes

TEACHER NOTES
- Discuss the two graphs. Ask students basic questions about the graphs to be sure that they read the graphs correctly.

- Have students write a story problem for each graph. Example: How many more children prefer peanut butter than prefer turkey? (9 children)

- Encourage students to share their story problems with their classmates.

EXTENSIONS
- Give the students an answer to a story problem. Have them use one of the graphs to make up a story problem to match the answer. For example:

  Answer: 4 children

  Problems: How many more children chose a cheese sandwich than a turkey sandwich? or

  How many more children lost 1 tooth than lost 3 or more teeth?

- Have the students write a story problem using one of the graphs in the handbook, *Math to Know*.

You may wish to use this **scoring rubric** to assess students' work.

3 points	• Student correctly reads and interprets both graphs. • Student correctly writes and solves 2 story problems that use data from the graphs.
2 points	• Student correctly reads and interprets both graphs. • Student correctly writes and solves 1 story problem that uses data from the graphs.
1 point	• Student does not correctly write a story problem that uses data from the graph.

Name _____ Date _____

Story Problems for Graphs

Write a story problem for each graph.

Favorite Sandwich

Peanut Butter

Cheese

Turkey

0 1 2 3 4 5 6 7 8 9 10

Number of children

Problem: _____

_____

Answer: _____

Children Who Lost Teeth in January

1 tooth	☺ ☺ ☺		
2 teeth	☺ ☺ ☺ ☺ ☺		
3 or more teeth	☺		

Key ☺ = 2 children

Problem: _____

_____

Answer: _____